HDQ

DATE DUE

APR 23 '01	OCT 7 '05	
APR 30 '01	7/8/06	
5-12		
JUL 11 '01		
OCT 11 '01		
OCT 18 '01		
DEC 27 '03		
NOV 1 3 2003		
MAY 1 '04		
MAY 1 7 2005		
JUN 0 7 2005		
JAN 2 6 2005		

GAYLORD   PRINTED IN U.S.A.

'20S & '30S
STYLE

'20S & '30S STYLE

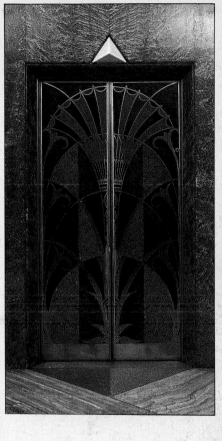

JG
PRESS

MICHAEL HORSHAM

A QUINTET BOOK

Published in the USA 1996 by JG Press.
Distributed by World Publications, Inc.

The JG Press imprint is a trademark of
JG Press, Inc.
455 Somerset Avenue
North Dighton, MA 02764

This edition produced for sale in the USA, its
territories and dependencies only.

ISBN 1-57215-171-4

This book was designed and produced by
Quintet Publishing Limited
6 Blundell Street
London N7 9BH

Creative Director: Peter Bridgewater
Art Director: Ian Hunt
Designer: Mike Morey
Project Editor: Judith Simons
Editor: Patricia Bayer
Picture Researcher: Ruth Sonntag

Typeset in Great Britain by
Central Southern Typesetters, Eastbourne
Manufactured in Hong Kong by
Regent Publishing Services Limited
Printed in Singapore by
Star Standard Industries (Pte) Ltd

CONTENTS

The Chrysler Building, New York, William van Alen, 1928–30.

AN APPROACH TO 1920s AND 1930s STYLE

If any one trend could be said to characterize the 1920s and 1930s, it must be the way in which innovation was constantly and rapidly transmuted into chic. The radical tendencies and advances in art, architecture and design were fast subsumed into the broader arena of public consumption, into such disparate or far-flung areas as transportation, politics and mass-communication.

Modernity became the watchword for the two decades, as with anything obviously old and out-moded rapidly superseded by the new and different. It was the age of streamlining, talking pictures and Franklin Roosevelt's New Deal. Dada, Surrealism and Constructivism grew up in response to the stagnancy of conventional art, and innovative new forms of architecture, chief among them Modernism, were embraced as the flagships and symbols of a new age. New and improved methods of communication – from the radio to the duplicating machine – worked their way into the lives of the masses, and new political theories found their voices and adherents. All these novelties – and many more – benefited from their newness in a world which increasingly came to demand new solutions for the problems of modern times.

Prior to the two decades in question, the West had effectively been destroyed by World War I. But cataclysm became a catalyst for fundamental change: in the postwar world, the desire for a fresh start, for a new epoch of progress and peace, became paramount.

World War I acted as a catalyst in other ways. The industrial world made advances far beyond those which would have been occasioned by five years of peacetime. Aeronautics, medicine and industrial chemistry benefited from the effects of the 'war to end all wars'. Industry itself had found that it needed to develop extremely efficient mass-production techniques in order to cope with demand. At the end of the war these were available to apply to the production of goods for the home. The boom in light industrial production was

● **LEFT** The De La Warr Pavilion, Bexhill-on-Sea, Mendelsohn & Chermayeff, 1935–36.
In its striking use of tubular steel and reinforced concrete, this spiral staircase displays many of the hallmarks of Modernist design.

●**ABOVE** Emile-Jacques Ruhlmann's *Hôtel d'un Collectionneur* at the 1925 Paris *Exposition Internationale des Arts Décoratifs et Industriels Modernes* (Pierre Patout, architect).
Pseudo-classical architectural forms housed the most luxurious modern furniture and *objets d'art* at the fair.

●**RIGHT** Zig Zag Chair, Gerrit Rietveld, 1934.
This design represents an important departure for Rietveld in the use of the diagonal. Until this point, the De Stijl movement had championed the use of the strict horizontal and vertical in its art and design aesthetic.

marked by the growth of firms such as Hoover, which employed production techniques it had learned in the process of waging war.

By the beginning of the 1920s the world had changed politically as well. In Germany the founding of the Weimar Republic in 1919 created a climate in which an institution such as the Bauhaus could operate. In Russia the founding of the Union of Soviet Socialist Republics also had its repercussions on a worldwide scale. Later, in Italy and Germany the rise of Fascism was set in opposition to the Communist ideal. The occurrence of the world economic recession, the great slump and the Wall Street Crash contributed to the political and economical cocktail which helped to create the unique character of the two decades in question.

Things were also changing in the home. In the United States, goods for domestic use, such as refrigerators and small electrical products, were made for, and more importantly, marketed to, a new mass of consumers. The 1920s and 1930s became the first age of the talented and eclectic industrial designer, whose wares could now be found in many homes.

These were goods aimed primarily at women, who were finding out that things were changing for them in many ways, too. While the men of the world had been away fighting for their countries, many women had had their first liberating taste of financial, and even social, independence. It is perhaps no coincidence, then, that another feature of the 1920s and 1930s was the growing emancipation of women. Dress became much less inhibiting, hair was cut fashionably short, powdering one's nose — and smoking — were allowed in public. Women were seen to alter the way in which they moved in the world. It was not so much that every woman radically altered her lifestyle, but at least in terms of popular mythology, the potential for change was seen to exist.

The habits of the average person changed, too, with the advent of the radio and talking pictures.

Home entertainment took on a new guise with regular networked radio shows, and the weekly trip to the movies greatly affected the ways in which people were to speak, look and act.

The 1920s and 1930s were truly international decades. Great international exhibitions at once aided the flow of ideas between continents, while paradoxically shoring up nationalistic tendencies. Once every four years the Olympics performed the same functions, showing the world national displays

● **OPPOSITE ABOVE** Four enamelled-ceramic vases, Boch Frères of Belgium, 1930s.

● **OPPOSITE BELOW** Greystone Hotel, Miami Beach, Florida, 1930s. Speed lines and a strong symmetry lend this building the look of marine architecture, redolent of the white-painted superstructure of an ocean liner.

● **RIGHT** Lobby of the Chrysler Building, New York, William van Alen, 1928–30. An imposing use of materials creates the opulence and grandeur necessary to maintain the corporate image of one of the car-manufacturing giants of the 1930s.

and international cooperation.

Unabashed novelty, chic modernity and constant change all played a part in the creation of the myriad styles, looks, products and ideas which characterize the 1920s and 1930s. The 20-year span includes many phenomena, from rising hemlines to streamlined trains, from Fred Astaire to Adolf Hitler, from glittering skyscrapers to plastic wireless sets – a never-ending list which serves to highlight both the differences and the common ground making up the things we recognize as distinctive examples of 1920s and 1930s style.

EXPERIENCE
+
EXPERIMENT = SUCCESS

Science and skill applied to everyday household equipment banish drudgery and make the daily task a pride and pleasure.

PARKINSON'S place over a century of experience at your service, but still they test and experiment and embody fresh discoveries in their appliances so that you may always have the Best.

Ask your local Gas Showroom to show you how, in the "NEW SUBURBIA" Cooker, Science enables you to control heat and to secure greater oven efficiency with reduced gas consumption.

Illustrated Booklet "P" sent free upon request.

THE PARKINSON 'NEW SUBURBIA' GAS COOKER

Parkinson 'New Suburbia' gas cooker, 1929.

CHAPTER ONE

CHANGE IN THE WORLD AND CHANGE IN THE HOME

The 1920s and 1930s were a period in history where extraordinary things occurred both on world stage and on the home front. With the benefit of hindsight it is a relatively simple task to pick out the significant objects, events and personalities. But we have a view of the 1920s and 1930s which is inevitably coloured by our experience of the world today, and it has become quite an easy task to ignore the mundane realities of day-to-day life then in favour of the bigger, more dramatic picture. The fact is that the lives of ordinary people were affected in very real terms by huge changes in the way the world was seen to work.

Politically and economically, there were huge shifts in the stability of nations, which were depending on the most powerful nation on earth, the United States, for the continuance of what seemed at times their very existence. There were few nations in the Western world which did not experience vast changes at the hands of politicians, who were busily attempting to determine the economic salvation of their respective countries.

Because of the economic supremacy enjoyed by the United States immediately after World War I, what happened there was inevitably felt in Europe. This was never more true than in the European reaction to the Wall Street Crash of 24 October 1929. The run up to the Crash had been characterized by the artificial boom which Americans had experienced from 1927 onwards. This was underpinned by massive borrowing against securities which were lacking in adequate coverage. When the integrity of the whole economic construction began to be doubted by the dealers and stockbrokers, a mass off-loading of what were assumed to be potentially ruinous holdings occurred. This atmosphere of panic built upon itself and on that fateful October day more than 13 million shares were sold. Five days later 16 million shares changed hands. Banks failed, fortunes were lost and the slump had begun.

The Wall Street Crash and the subsequent financial chaos came at the worst possible time for Europe. The continent was in the midst of post-World War I reconstruction, and some of its nations were particularly reliant on American aid – among them Germany. The Weimar Republic had been set up in 1919 in the eponymous city on the banks of the River Ilm (in what is now East Germany). Under the presidency of Friedrich Ebert, a middle-of-the-road socialist, there was a real attempt made to organize the Republic along democratic lines.

The new state was hampered from the outset by the burden of reparations payments to be made under the terms of the Armistice. Furthermore, hyper-inflation was running out of control, a condition which eventually led to a collapse of the financial structure, hence limiting the chances of success

for the liberal, and in some ways forward-thinking, Weimar-controlled country. The inflation which hit Germany at this time saw the Deutschmark decrease in worth to 100,000th of its prewar value. At the height of its inflationary period (1922–23), a simple bus ticket could cost as much as 150,000 million marks! Recovery of sorts from this situation was heralded and to an extent underwritten by the United States, in the shape of the Dawes Plan. This was the title given to a report which was acted upon by the American administration and which came into effect in 1924. The basis of the Dawes Plan was a system of loans intended to assist Germany in stabilizing its economy through the reorganization of the Reichsbank. In addition to this, the loans were intended to help Germany meet the obligations incurred by the Armistice treaty.

The years 1924 to 1929 saw a time of relative stability, a condition that does not seem to have been difficult to achieve, given the wildly oscillating fortunes of world economics on either side of this brief five-year period. When the Wall Street Crash occurred it served to open the way for realignment in political thought and action all over the world. Europe was thrown into further monetary disarray with the collapse of the Austrian Credit Anstalt Bank. This was seen as a direct result of the slump occasioned by the Crash on the other side of the Atlantic.

By 1930 more than five million people were out of work in Germany, and in September of that year

Adolf Hitler had his first electoral success. By 1933 Hitler had risen to the post of Vice-Chancellor. The burning of the Reichstag was followed by the elimination of his erstwhile rivals and on 2 August 1934 Hitler was proclaimed Führer of the Third Reich.

In the United States, where this world slump had been kicked into action, the Republicans found themselves out of office. The dynasty of Harding, Coolidge and Hoover, the three Republican presidents since the war, was ended by the election of Democrat Franklin Delano Roosevelt. These years were in large part shaped by Roosevelt's New Deal. This was a selection of economic and social reforms intended to turn around the nation's fortunes and, by association, those of the other countries dependent on the United States for their economic good health. Moreover, as a plan it was designed to help end both the financial uncertainty

● **RIGHT** Hitler at the opening of the first Volkswagen plant in 1938. The 'people's car' was built to run on the newly constructed *Autobahns*. Both were symptomatic of the change in the fortunes of Germany under Hitler's uncompromising rule.

and unemployment which dogged the American industrial sector. Such were the liberal, socially concerned elements of later parts of the plan that it met with some resistance from American industrialists, who saw schemes for the Social Security of workers as undermining their positions and, worse, perhaps opening the door to Communist influence.

In spite of this, the plan met with some success. Between the years 1933 and 1941 over two million Americans were employed on reforestation projects and four million were found work on the huge public-works initiatives comprising the construction of dams, hydroelectric power stations and highways. Part two of the New Deal introduced the

aforementioned Social Security schemes and ushered in the beginnings of a guarantee system for small farmers, whose experience of the dust-bowl years from the mid-1930s had led to migrations to the west in search of work and a new life.

In Britain, 1929 saw the defeat of the Conservative government under Stanley Baldwin and the election of a socialist government under Ramsay MacDonald. The economic crisis, exacerbated by the Crash and slump, affected Britain, too, so much so that by 1931 a coalition government had to be formed to handle affairs of state. The so-called 'National' government continued under Baldwin until 1935, when Neville Chamberlain stepped in. This was a time of growing instability for Britain, further underlined by the 1936 abdication of Edward VIII in order to spend the rest of his days with the love of his life, the American divorcée, Wallis Simpson.

In Italy under Mussolini, as in Germany under Hitler, Fascism had taken hold. Spain underwent a bloody civil war which also resulted in a Fascist government taking control. In Russia, Lenin had died and Joseph Stalin had begun to administer his own brand of autocratic rule, introducing the first of the Five-Year Plans. The decades between the two world wars had seen the world largely polarized into nations which were either broadly right or left wing. Nationalism prevailed under the guise of self-preservation. Many commentators of the time watched Germany undergo its *Wirtschaftswunder* (economic miracle) and admired Hitler; others viewed his expansionist tendencies and avowed anti-Semitism with increasing alarm.

In this 20-year period the world moved from war to pece and then to the brink of war again. The period of peace was an extraordinarily turbulent and complex one, but against this backdrop the ordinary lives of people continued both in and out of their homes. The lives of people in the 1920s and 1930s were obviously affected by the bigger events. Wages in inflationary Germany were taken home in wheelbarrows, and the economic upheaval caused the Jarrow shipyards to be closed, resulting in hunger marches to London. Across the Atlantic, another kind of revolution was underway. Certainly, mass unemployment and financial instability affected the lives of millions of people there, soup kitchens and dole queues being as much a feature of American life as anywhere else. But in spite of this, there was still a consumer-led boom which occurred as the American economy began to recover, advertising went to work (as did its designers) and people began to consume more goods than ever before.

Raymond Loewy's 'Coldspot' refrigerator for Sears, Roebuck, which first appeared in 1935, is one example of an escalating demand by the

N° 96. — 4 Décembre 1920.
26ᵉ ANNÉE

France et Colonies   Étranger
Trois mois...   9.50   10.   »
Six mois.....   18.   »   19.50
Un an........   35.   »   38.   »

Les abonnements partent du 1ᵉʳ de chaque mois.

75 Centimes

F. JUVEN, éditeur
1, rue de Choiseul, 1
PARIS
Tout changement d'adresse doit être accompagné de 50 centimes.

Copyright 1920 by LE RIRE, Paris

Le Rire

JOURNAL HUMORISTIQUE PARAISSANT LE SAMEDI

TOTOTE EST CONSERVATRICE

— Moi, ma petite, je suis féministe.
— Eh bien ! pas moi : j'aime mieux les hommes.

Dessin de F. FABIANO.

● **LEFT** The Cord '810'. A design representative of the stylish, gadget-laden upper end of the automobile market, where styling and superb performance were expensive to buy, but in certain circles absolutely necessary.

American public for a new breed of home product. In the five years from its launch, sales climbed from around 15,000 per year to an estimated 275,000. It was of course in the nature of the self-promoting designer to claim that the responsibility for the increase lay with the improvements in the design of the object, but there were other factors involved. Apart from the increased availability of electrical appliances and supplies to ordinary homes, the rise in the consumption of goods of this type was assisted by other changes. The growth of advertising and the media, together with the appearance of credit terms or hire purchase, made the buying of new things easier than before for those on average wages. One thing the designers of consumer goods did do was to make each successive model slightly different from the last. These 'improvements' sometimes enhanced the performance of the machine, but often they were cosmetic, employed to fuel the desire for an annual model change in what was rapidly becoming a saturated market.

Similarly, in the world of automobile transport the yearly model change took over as the motive behind soaring sales. In the early 1920s the most common car around had been the Ford Model 'T', some 15 million having been sold since its launch. General Motors usurped its rival's unargued supremacy with the introduction of a more stylish car for a similar price, and for the first time since Henry Ford had cornered the market in the family car, real competition for a share in what was by now a mass market ensued. The growth in the 'styling' end of automobile production is underlined by the fact that in 1928 Harley T Earl was appointed head of the Art and Color Section, of General Motors; by the end of the next decade the division was known as the Styling Section, and by the 1950s Earl found fame as the prime mover behind the ever-changing yearly fashion for bigger and bigger fins on GM cars. Although the art of automotive styling is said to have reached its apotheosis in the 1950s, the interwar years saw many noticeable examples of the car stylist's art. It was a skill applied purely for the purpose of selling the car, positioning it within a mass market and capitalizing on the public's desire for something undeniably modern, a car which said something about its owner and which could easily be bought.

The Cord Company started in the United States just before the Depression, and at this point in history was doing reasonably well. In the post-depression years an attempt to move into the luxury car market was obviously mistimed, seriously undermined as it was by the effects of the slump. The car with which they had hoped to grab a share of the lucrative luxury market was the two seater L29 which, selling at over $3,000, was almost doomed from the start. The failure of the L29 forced the Cord Company out of business but by 1935 Cord was back with a car which was to become a classic of interwar design. The Cord '810' was modernity incarnate: the teardrop-shaped mud-guards held rectractable headlamps and the char-acteristic horizontal dynamic of the chrome speed lines on the wraparound radiator grille made the car a striking object to look at. Due to the power wielded by the 'Big Three' motor-car companies – Ford, Chrysler and General Motors – the Cord could not compete and sold poorly. By 1939, the Cord Company was out of business yet again, this time permanently.

Striking car though it was, the Cord was up against the muscle of the big car-producing com-panies, which had become adept at advertising their products in the glossy magazines and on the radio. In 1924, responding once more to the change in status occurring for some women, Ford advertised their closed sedan as 'suitable for the business woman who wishes to expedite her affairs'. The imagery in the advertisement was a subtle mixture of modernity and domesticity, showing a young, fashionably attired woman on the telephone with a Ford Sedan parked outside her suitably curtained window. By 1935, the Ford 'V8' was being adver-

● BELOW The Ford Model 'T'.
Henry Ford's people's car; the Model 'T' represented the first affordable family car and heralded changes in everything from production technique to mass-marketing.

tised as 'a symbol of progress and the newest, latest developments in Automobile building'.

Pierce-Arrow, with its up-market aspirations, would display cars in magazine advertisements beneath incongruous pictures of dining tables set with cut crystal, fine bone china and candelabra. Buick allied itself to the glamour of Hollywood, showing a still from the *Gold Diggers of 1935*, with Dick Powell sitting in a Buick flanked by at lest 50 beautiful girls, all of whom appear to be playing white grand pianos! The gushing copy of the advertisement proclaimed that the car 'harmonises perfectly with the advanced and newly created styles which Warner Brothers Productions display'. Clearly product placement within films is nothing new and neither is the associative power of advertising.

The predilection for domestic appliances continued to grow through the 1920s, as electricity became available to more homes. These products were made more desirable, and therefore more consumable, first by dint of the jobs they could do and, secondarily, by their design or styling characteristics. For instance, the now-familiar pistol-shaped hairdryer made its first appearance in the 1920s. Electric toasters, kettles and curling tongs, all of which had been around for at least a decade, became everyday items, only their novelty value now shifted from the fact that they were powered by electricity to the way they looked. Production methods were increasingly geared towards mass-production for escalating markets, and the distinctively shaped objects we now think of as being characteristic of 1920s and 1930s style were stamped, pressed or rolled out of the raw materials from which they were made in massive quantities.

The labour-saving home became more of an issue to the American people as hygiene and efficiency were promoted as virtues by the manufacturers of goods and newly professionalized home economists. In 1932 Norman Bel Geddes styled the 'Oriole' stove for the Standard Gas Equipment Corporation of New York. It was notable for the smooth lines of its body work, facilitating mass manufacture, filling the need to look modern and easing the subsequent cleaning it would undergo by its proud new owner. In 1936 the Hoover Manufacturing Company brought out the 'Hoover Junior', an upright vacuum cleaner with twin revolving brushes driven by a belt attached to the motor and to a 'beating' mechanism. It was sold with the advertising slogan 'beats as it cleans'.

With the advent of radio as a mass medium in the early 1920s, and the subsequent establishment of the Radio Corporation of America (RCA), the Columbia Broadcasting System (CBS) and National Broadcasting Corporation (NBC), the opportunity for networking came into view. Furthermore, national radio advertising and sponsorship became possible

● **RIGHT** Hoover vacuum cleaner, 1929.
Prior to the advent of 'styling' by industrial designers, domestic appliances like the Hoover were nothing if not functional in appearance.

● **OPPOSITE** Page from Harrods catalogue, 1929.
Further examples of the nature of the new electrical appliances which could be bought for the home.

ELECTRICAL DEPARTMENT
Household Electric Appliances.   Please State Voltage When Ordering

'MAGNET' ELECTRIC IRON
This Iron is fitted with a thumb rest, and the handle and handle support are specially designed to ensure a comfortable grip Supplied with six feet of flex and adaptor
Weight 4 lbs., 350 watts **16/-**
Weight 5½ lbs., 450 watts **17/6**

'MAGNET' UNIVERSAL ELECTRIC IRON
An Iron for use on voltages from 100 to 125 and from 200 to 250 volts. Easily detachable handle allows compact packing for travelling. Complete with stand and six feet of flex and adaptor. Weight 3 lbs., 300 watts .. **22/6**

'MAGNET' ELECTRIC KETTLE
Ensures boiling water in a few minutes. Polished copper, tinned inside, and mounted on heat insulating feet. Has device to prevent lid falling when tilted

2 pints size.	650 watts	..	..	..	**26/-**
3 " "	900 "	..	..	..	**32/-**
6 " "	1400 "	..	..	..	**52/-**

'MAGNET' SHAVING POT
An electric shaving pot with bowl of seamless copper, heavily nickel-plated Heats water ready for shaving in two or three minutes. Mounted on heat insulating feet .. **25/-**

'MAGNET' ELECTRIC MILK STERILIZER
A milk sterilizer and food warmer, with china inner container. A real boon in the nursery. Has two circuits, one for boiling and one for simmering
1 pint. 500 watts .. **50/-**

'MAGNET' COFFEE PERCOLATOR
A Nickel-plated Coffee Percolator mounted on heat insulating feet. The Interior Percolator Chamber is easily removable to facilitate cleaning. Packed in a carton complete with connector
1½ pints **35/-**
2½ " **38/-**

'MAGNET' WATER BOILER
A Water Boiler, designed to boil a small quantity of water speedily. Made in two sizes, and finished polished copper or nickel-plated. Mounted on heat insulating feet. Packed in carton complete with connector
Polished Copper .. ½ pint, 28/6 ; 1 pint 31/6
Nickel-plated .. .. ½ " 30/- ; 1 " 35/-

'MAGNET' ELECTRIC TOASTER
Toasts two slices of bread simultaneously in approximately three minutes. Side finger pieces and the feet are heat insulated. Can be used on the breakfast table. Perforated top permits toast already made to be kept hot. Finished nickel-plate
600 watts **25/-**

Purchases value 10/- and over are sent Post Free in England and Wales

HARRODS have all the newest types of Electrical Appliances. Full particulars on request

'MAGNET' GRILLER AND TOASTER
Very light in weight but extremely serviceable. This combined Griller and Toaster has a grid top which permits of its use as a boiling or simmering table. Constructed of sheet metal, stove black enamelled, with top part enamelled grey. Three heat control Complete with Grill, Pan and Grid **£3 5 0**

'MAGNET' ELECTRIC TOWEL RAIL
Towel Rail of one inch copper tubing—nickel-plated. Provided with combined filler and safety valve. Complete with connector .. **£7 15 0**

'MAGNET' ELECTRIC SEWING MACHINE MOTOR
Suitable for driving any domestic or treadle machine. Affixed by single screw. Belt driven. Motor of universal type suitable for use on either direct or alternating current **£5 5 0**

'MAGNET' ELECTRIC CLEANER
This electric cleaner, entirely British made, is supplied complete with a number of useful attachments." It will perform a great deal of household work in a better and quicker way than any other method, gathering up every particle of dust and dirt from floors, walls and furniture. It pays for itself many times over in the household labour it saves. Price (complete with all attachments) .. **£12 12 0**

'MAGNET' ELECTRIC HOT PLATE
A small circular hot plate, nickel-plated, with heat insulating feet, designed for table use. Can be used in a lighting circuit
500 watts **24/-**

'MAGNET' BOILING PLATE
A quick boiling plate with cast iron base and polished grid. Will serve many useful purposes 1000 watts **27/6**

ALL PRICES ARE SUBJECT TO MARKET FLUCTUATIONS

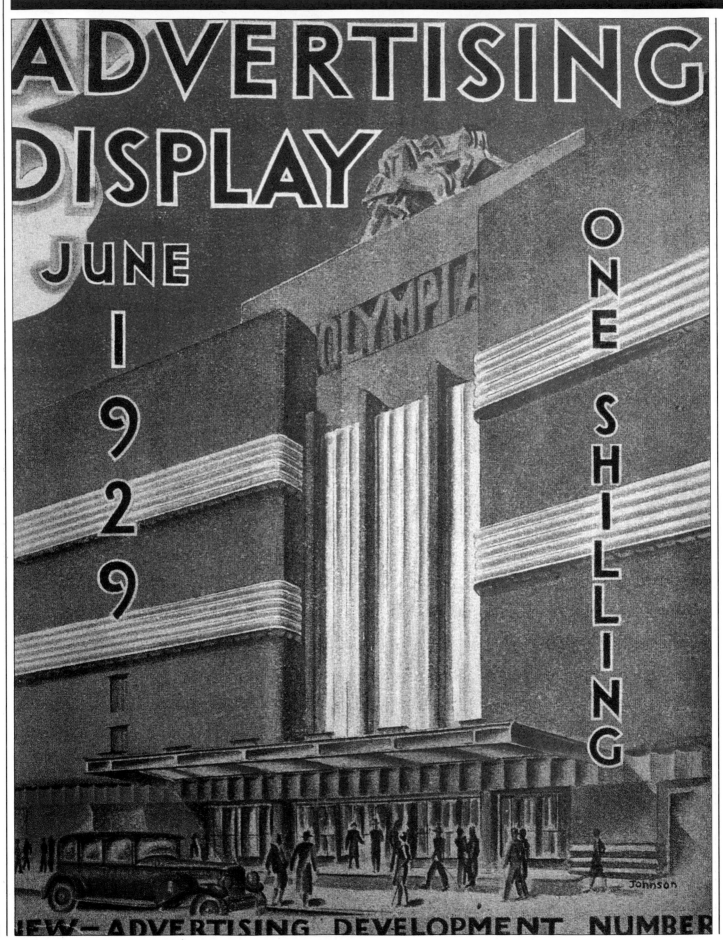

ADVERTISING DISPLAY
JUNE 1 1929

OLYMPIA

ONE SHILLING

Johnson

NEW — ADVERTISING DEVELOPMENT NUMBER

● **OPPOSITE** Front cover of *Advertising Display* magazine, 1929. This journal catered to those involved in the rapidly growing advertising business. It is particularly interesting as it shows the front façade of Joseph Emberton's monumental Olympia Exhibition Halls of 1929–30.

● **RIGHT** Pye Model 'K' wireless receiver, 1932. Displaying the idealized 'sunray' motif which covered the 'new suburbia', this radio set has become a classic 1930s icon.

for the first time. To estimate the impact of this on the American public would take a book in itself but, as more and more homes acquired a radio set, so the potential audience for advertisers grew alongside a proportionate upturn in consumer consumption of goods and services.

If there is one thing which characterizes the new designs of the consumer durables of the interwar years, particularly in the United States, it is the encasement of the working parts in a smoothly modern housing. Stylistically, this trend served to underline modernity by bringing the goods into line with the broadly held functionalist theories used to legitimate the work of the industrial designers of this age. But as has already been mentioned, ease of manufacture was a strongly determinant factor in the way things began to look by the 1930s. However, this was not necessarily the case in other parts of the world.

In Germany at the time of the rise of Nazism, and in line with that country's nationalist philosophies, the 'volks' range of goods was brought out as a state-funded exercise in mass-manufacture and -consumption. Radio grew in Germany only slightly later than it did in the United States, partly due to the fact that Goebbels, acting as head propagandist for the Nazis, realized the medium's potential for reaching the masses. Consequently, over a million *Volksempfänger* (literally, 'people's radio sets') were sold very cheaply to the public after 1934, enabling Hitler to speak to his people as a nation and expound national socialist philosophies in a more potent way than ever before.

In Britain, too, the BBC began to broadcast, paving the way for the escalation in the popularity of radio as a means of entertainment in the 1930s. Radio sets became as much a part of the British home as chairs and tables, and indeed their appearance could be either as furniture, clad in veneered-wood cabinets, or as functional architect-designed radio sets, produced from combinations of wood or from the newer plastics. By 1936 the BBC had begun the first High Definition Television Broadcasting service from Alexandra Palace (although the TV set was to remain a rarity in British homes until well after World War II).

As has been shown, the growth in consumer goods in the 1920s and 1930s was set against a rapidly changing world, both politically and economically. On the one hand, people's lives were changed by the shifts in economic power occurring on a global scale, while on the other they were altered by the things they were able to buy. Consequently, it was during the 1920s and 1930s that two phenomena we well understand and daily experience today – that of the 'mass consumer' and that of the 'mass advertiser' – really came into being for the first time.

Chrysler 'Airflow', 1935.

CHAPTER TWO

STREAMFORM, SPEED AND THE SEARCH FOR SUPERMAN

The publication of Norman Bel Geddes' *Horizons* in 1932 came in the middle of another quintessentially modern age. The 1920s and 1930s were, to a large extent, characterized by world economic upheaval and national instability, together with the growth of the first global mass markets. Much of the production of industrial designers like Bel Geddes (1893–1958), together with the studios of Raymond Loewy (1893–1986), Henry Dreyfuss (1904–72), Harold Van Doren (1895–1957) and Walter Dorwin Teague (1883–1960), was inspired by a readily perceived demand for rationalization in design. The results could then be employed to capitalize upon the search for consumer goods and services, the need for positive national and corporate identities, and the desire for a fresh start.

In addition to this, efficiency and speed came to be seen as watchwords for modernity. The growth of the phenomenon of sleek and elliptical streamforming or streamlining, particularly in the 1930s, is evidence of this preoccupation.

Aircraft were an obvious area of design to which streamlining techniques could be applied. The boat seen in plan bears the 'teardrop' shape, which is the essence of streamlined design. Therefore, the transition between the boat that flies and the aero-plane that cuts through the air with greater ease is, with hindsight, not a difficult link to forge. However, the technological leaps to be made between the boxy biplane and the seamless sleek monoplane were greater than may first appear. Less drag means greater speed, greater speed means greater stress and, therefore, while the principles of aerodynamic flight were understood, progress in this arena relied on the development of stronger and lighter alloys such as aluminium. Once the technological breakthroughs had been made progress was fast, from DC3 to jet engines in a decade.

The Douglas DC3 had become fully streamlined and operational by 1935, the same year Le Corbusier had spoken of aircraft as being emblematic of 'the new age' in his piece entitled *Aircraft*. The teardrop shape was, although not newly discovered, newly employed as a design solution for aerodynamic and stylistic problems. Some of the objects to which this hybrid of stylistic and scientific invention was applied benefited from the use of the characteristic streamform shape. For others, it was enough to command the association with the newly desirable, modern characteristic of speed through the use of streamlined shapes. Thus the design studios of Teague, Loewy, Dreyfuss and Harold van Doren

● **LEFT** Douglas DC3, flying under TWA banner. This aircraft first entered service in 1936, subsequent to this over 11,000 of the type were built, making it the most successful commercial aircraft ever.

● **LEFT** *Supermarine S6B, R J Mitchell, 1931.*
In the search for speed, air races provided the proving ground for national attempts in gaining air speed records. Technological advances were forced through the heat of competition for the Schneider trophy.

● **BELOW** Hudson 4-6-4 locomotive.
This streamlined engine was designed by Henry Dreyfuss in 1938 for pulling the 'Twentieth Century Limited'.

(the big four, but by no means the only successful industrial designers in the United States between the wars) would use the streamline motif, the characteristic teardrop shape, for its associative powers as much as its aerodynamic qualities. So at this time, such things as a streamlined baby carriage or a streamlined desk stapler could be found – such

was the idea of modernity connected with the idea of speed.

Steam locomotives in particular saw an increase in efficiency and speed. Transport companies seized the opportunity for the realization of corporate identity in its most apposite form. In the United States, Henry Dreyfuss's train, the 'Twentieth Cen-

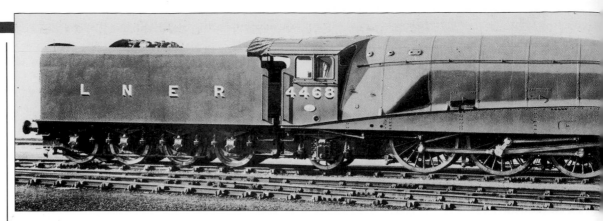

● **RIGHT** LNER 'A4' Pacific locomotive with streamlined cladding, Sir Nigel Gresley, 1935.
The fastest steam locomotive ever built, in 1938 the 'A4' engine called *Mallard* set a record of 126 mph (202.7 km/h).

● **BELOW** LMS Pacific locomotive with streamlined cladding, Oliver Vaughan Snell Bulleid, 1937.
A striking corporate image and proven advances in fuel economy were gained through this innovative design.

tury Limited', which ran for the Pennsylvania Transport Company from 1938, contributed both to the cult of the designer and the corporate identity of the railroad company. In Great Britain, too, the designs of Sir Nigel Gresley and his contemporary, Oliver Vaughan Snell Bulleid, contributed first to the efficiency of their locomotives and, secondly, to the opportunity for a striking corporate image. That efficiency and therefore speed were increased is beyond doubt: the record set for a steam locomotive of 126 mph (202.7 km/h) by Gresley's 'Mallard' in 1938 still stands.

The 'Coronation Scot', Bulleid's contribution to the art of streamlining, was sent on a tour of the United States in 1937 and, although the sending of a streamlined train to America may appear to be something of a 'coals to Newcastle' exercise, the fact that this was a coronation year in Great Britain underlined the nationalistic elements of the event. Similarly, the vision of New Deal America was compounded by the heroic vision of the designers of pan-American means of travel. Through the nature of its products, the United States could be seen to be leaving behind the more turbulent years of the late 1920s and heading, very determinedly, into the future.

When it was introduced in 1934, the Chrysler 'Airflow' car was a truly modern automobile, in that it incorporated streamform styling of a quasi-scientific origin. The fact that the vehicle failed to set light to the public imagination has been attributed to several factors, not least the recession which had hit the United States by mid-1937. Furthermore, the fact the car was too far beyond contemporary experience of what a car should look like did not help the public to accept its shape. Nevertheless, the modernity of the car was never in question, and although it was withdrawn by 1938, by this time the streamform was often seen in the exterior styling of the American motor car.

As in the case of the stapler and the baby carriage, streamforming was applied to products which simply did not need to be able to cut through the air with greater efficiency; there are examples of streamlined meat slicers and even manure spreaders.

The 'Coldspot' Refrigerator, designed by the Raymond Loewy studio for the Sears, Roebuck company from 1934 onwards featured, and was advertised as having, 'automotive styling' (indeed there were reasons for this, as the controlling interests in the firms producing refrigerators were often in the hands of the major American car manufacturers). The techniques used for rolling the sheet metal into the shapes for the cars on Route 66 were transposed onto the manufacture of a fashionable icebox. As the yearly model change of car began to take hold, so did the yearly model

● **RIGHT**
BELOW Duesenberg 'SJ' convertible, Fred Duesenberg, 1933. This was one of the most expensive and opulent cars produced in the USA during the 1920s and 1930s. Coachbuilt and engineered to exacting standards, this car would cost upwards of $15,000.

change of refrigerator, with minute styling differences making this year's model more acceptable and so much more desirable than the last.

Clearly, streamlining was a phenomenon which transcended the purely functional and, like Art Deco, it became a name for yet another form of applied decoration. Moreover, in transcending the functional the streamform became a symbolic expression of a new age of efficiency and speed – an age in which the forward thrust of intellectual thought expressed in art and architecture was borne faster forward by hunger for the modernity of a newly designed world. It is surely no coincidence that this period in history spawned the ultimate superhero, Superman, and the lesser but avidly followed Buck Rogers, a traveller in outer space, no less! Superman was sought after as an icon for the future, but the true icons, perhaps the true supermen of America at this point in its history, were to be found in the design studios. Objects, artefacts, trains, planes and automobiles were restyled during these years to represent a vision of the future which was at once desirable and attainable. From the 1920s, when vast airships plied across the Atlantic and across the United States, to the 1930s, when air travel took on the trappings of speed and safety with which it is associated today, the forms realized by the designers and stylists of this era were nothing if not modernistic. Such was the shift towards modernity in all areas of design at this

time that it is perhaps fair to say that there was a feeling among some of the design fraternity that, in terms of man's ingenuity in triumphing over nature, anything was possible. The view was distinctly towards the future and the service which could be provided by man's technological mastery. Witness the images to be found in Norman Bel Geddes' *Horizons,* including massive aircraft, streamlined ships and cars, and all manner of forward-looking novelty.

The designs by Bel Geddes for *Horizons* are distinctly futuristic, and it was a theme to be found in Le Corbusier's plans for his 'Radiant City'. However, the utopian futurism expressed by the design world was not allowed to take over. This was a kind of modernity echoed rather more darkly in Fritz Lang's epic 1926 film, *Metropolis.* Likewise, the 1936 production of *Things to Come* showed the flip side of the utopian dream of the new world. Charlie Chaplin, too, had a point to make in *Modern Times,* also from 1936, which satirized the rise of the *ubermensch* (Superman) and championed the 'little man'.

Indeed, the day-to-day life of ordinary people all over the world must have made the dreams of Bel Geddes and Le Corbusier seem very distant, if 'Joe Average' was even aware of them. Although the lives of many people were eased in small ways by the impact of new technology on their worlds – in the shape of electric lights and radio, cars and trains – the search for Superman was in effect a search for escape. For the average person 'Superman' would therefore be more likely to be seen in the shape of Clark Gable or James Cagney than Le Corbusier or Raymond Loewy. In terms of the ordinary man or woman the search for the superheroes of this era was undoubtedly helped by the fact that the 1920s and 1930s were an age of unparalleled, unprecedented mass entertainment.

● **LEFT** Hoover Model 262, 1939.
The vacuum cleaner in this promotional photograph sports a somewhat futuristic head and a smart-looking bag.

● **ABOVE RIGHT** Model of a streamlined bus, Norman Bel Geddes, 1939.
This is but one of Bel Geddes' visionary designs, whose 'teardrop' shapes were meant to take advantage of low wind resistance as well as to cut down on fuel.

● **RIGHT** Futuristic film still from *Things to Come,* 1936.

He stands alone as the greatest entertainer of modern times! No one on earth can make you laugh as heartily or touch your heart as deeply...the whole world laughs, cries and thrills to his priceless genius!
Charlie Chaplin
in
MODERN TIMES
Written, Directed and Produced by Charles Chaplin
Released thru United Artists

CHAPTER THREE

THE NEW MASS MEDIA: FROM THE WIRELESS AND TALKIES, TO THE JUKEBOX AND JAZZ

In 1937 the Chrysler Corporation ran an advertisement in a nationally distributed magazine for one of its many automobiles; in small lettering under the picture of the car were the words 'Tune in on Major Burnes, CBS every Thursday 9–10 pm Eastern Standard Time'. This advertisement is significant for two main reasons: it represented the extent of networking and therefore the size of audience that radio was reaching at this time, and it reflected American radio's reliance on sponsorship. In the United States, the power of advertisements to influence the consumption patterns of an eager nation became inextricably linked to radio broadcasts from the earliest times. Radio institutions like the Kraft Music Hall were interdependent on the success of the sponsor's famous dairy products and the success of the medium. It is impossible to determine which, Kraft or the radio, owed its continued success to which. However, the popularity of radio and its astounding growth all over the world between the wars had come from relatively inauspicious beginnings.

As early as 1915, the American Telegraph and Telephone Company had managed to broadcast speech and music over a distance of 4,800 miles (7,680 km). Consequently, the United States led the way in the development and application of radio broadcasting technology. It was not until 1922 that Great Britain was to begin broadcasting on a regular, non-amateur basis.

Hannen Swaffer, a reporter on the London *Daily Graphic,* on viewing a 1921 copy of the New York *Morning Telegraph,* is reported to have been amazed to see two whole pages of radio broadcast listings, covering every subject from 'opera to wheat prices'. Such was his amazement that he was prompted to write an article about the spread of this new American phenomenon. The words he wrote on the 'new' medium of entertainment subsequently became the front-page story in the London *Evening News.* The story was taken up by other papers, notably the *Daily Mail* and the *Weekly Despatch.* Paradoxically, the news of radio was spread in Great Britain by means of the newspaper. Within weeks of this story breaking, and, so it is rumoured, partially in response to the excitement generated by the news of the depth of American involvement in radio, the British Broadcasting Company was set up under the aegis of the Post Office. It began regular broadcasts and subsequently was incorporated as the British Broadcasting Corporation, under Lord Reith.

Obviously, the United States was far ahead in its exploitation of the medium. The first commercial broadcasting service, Western Electric KFDK, had been set up in 1920. Commercial radio expanded rapidly in the country and was largely dependent on the uptake of the medium as a viable proposition

● **LEFT** Philips 930A wireless, 1930.
One of the first local receivers to incorporate speaker and radio in one tabletop cabinet. Millions were produced but, sadly, few survive today.

● **BELOW LEFT** Rogers 'Majestic', 1935.
A model designed to stand in the corner of the room as a large piece of furniture-cum-entertainment-centre.

by companies wishing to advertise. Because of the commercial nature of American broadcasts, the production values attached to programmes soared as companies vied with each other for audiences and the revenue they would generate from advertising. Consequently, the competitive nature of broadcasting in the United States meant that while techniques of production and technology were surging forward in an effort to attract and hold more and more listeners, the content of radio was geared towards pure entertainment. Therefore, trivia became the staple diet of the listening public.

Commercially led radio in the 1930s, particularly in the United States, was fuelled by comedies, quizzes, dance bands, light music and the nascent 'soap opera'. The 'soaps' were so named because, as a form of entertainment, they first saw the light of day as cliffhanging dramas sponsored by the major soap and detergent manufacturers. Aimed at the American housewife, they were designed to get her hooked on one story and, theoretically at least, on one brand of soap powder. The name of the company would be liberally sprinkled, like the powder, throughout the programme. The cliffhanging ending was often employed, and the desire to attract audiences – and to increase sponsor's sales – led to some decidedly odd examples of the genre. One such 1930s soap, *Light of the World*, took a moral, Midwestern stance in recounting biblical tales. One episode was met with incredulity by its audience when the announcer, at the end of the latest gripping episode, gravely posed the question: 'Did Eve do wrong????'

On the other hand, there were definite quality programmes, which were the best of their kind in the world. The radio careers of George Burns and Gracie Allen, Bing Crosby, Bob Hope and Rudy Vallee all took off in the 1930s as the demand for radio entertainment continued to grow. One of the more bizarre offshoots of American radio comedy in the 1930s was the occurrence of the radio ventriloquist. Since ventriloquy involves visual deception, the phenomenal success of Edgar Bergen and his puppets, Charlie McCarthy and Mortimer Snerd, remains a mystery, but happen it did.

The success of the American radio companies can be measured by the fact that by the outbreak of war in 1939, there were over 900 operative radio stations and four national networks. New York alone could boast 20 radio stations.

● **BELOW** BBC Broadcasting House, London (Val Myers, 1931).
The hub of British broadcasting. Both Wells Coates and Serge Chermayeff contributed to the design of its interior fittings.

Radio grew in Britain, too, with the establishment of the BBC in 1922. However, founder Lord Reith was seen to shy away from the American system of commercial sponsorship for programmes. Instead he preferred to opt for a licensing system. This meant that, during the 1920s and '30s, the production values behind BBC radio were not as high as those on American commercial radio and for many years the BBC suffered from an amateurishness (which the listeners, knowing no better, never complained about). By the end of the 1930s BBC radio attracted over 15 million listeners every night.

Indeed, the power of radio was wielded politically as well as dramatically, as two of its famous users illustrated. Firstly, Goebbels, Hitler's Minister for Propaganda, acknowledged the medium as being as important a communicative tool for the Third Reich as the printing press was for Napoleon, and he proceeded to exploit it relentlessly. Secondly, in 1938 the Mercury Theater, under the direction of the brilliant *enfant terrible,* Orson Welles, staged a radio production of H G Wells' *The War of The Worlds.* The production consisted of light music regularly interrupted by news reports that Martians had landed in the United States. The reports of the subsequent panic and belief in the possibility of Martian invasion are well known and demonstrate the efficacy of the radio as the most immediate communicative device known to the world during the 1920s and 1930s. Whether listening on headphones to the crystal set of the early 1920s or grouped in armchairs around the 'piece of furniture' in the corner of every living room, for many people all over the world radio and the radio set represented a pivotal part of life. It served not only to entertain but to contribute to the feeling that the ordinary listener was part of a very modern world, which was linked and at times characterized by the phenomenon that was 'the wireless'.

If the wireless represented home entertainment in the 1920s and 1930s then going out to be entertained came more and more to rely on one particular medium during those two decades. That medium, of course, was film. The movies, already big business by the start of the 1920s, experienced a rapid growth through that decade and into the next. The silent movie had reached its apotheosis with productions like D W Griffith's *Birth of a Nation* in 1915 and *Intolerance* in 1916. These blockbusting films set trends for high production values in dramatically oriented silent films. Movies also offered an opportunity for the cross-fertilization of ideas in art and imagery on a worldwide scale. The German director Ernst Lubitsch was influenced by his country's Expressionist movement in art and his films reflected this, with their sets displaying stark angularity, dark shadows and strong Expressionist imagery.

When Samuel Goldwyn imported the 1919 German film, *The Cabinet of Dr Caligari* (directed by Robert Wiene), into Hollywood and then the rest of the country in 1921, it was a huge success, opening the door for other European directors to have their films seen by a wider audience. Film began to represent yet another facet of global communication, one which had hitherto remained unexploited on any kind of large scale. With silent film there was no language barrier, and the ideas and characteristics of nations were fed through the medium to other countries. For example, Fritz Lang's famous vision of the future, *Metropolis* (1926), was inspired by Lang's first visit to New York. It was subsequently re-fed to New York as a vision of a future through distinctly German eyes. Lang was seen to continue this trend of social commentary in his *The Testament of Dr Mabuse,* made in 1932. This film was said to be an allegory for the process of terrorism practised by Hitler in Germany.

The crosscurrents of internationalism in film were continued with Ernst Lubitsch directing the all-American Mary Pickford in *Rosita* in 1923, in which the German brought distinctly European style to bear on possibly one of the most famous faces in the United States. Mary Pickford's husband, Douglas Fairbanks, had by this time become renowned for a new genre of movie, the swashbuckler, in which a story set against a faintly plausible, though inaccurate, historical background would be played out using magnificently imaginative stunts and sets. Between the years 1921 and 1926, Fairbanks made *The Three Musketeers, Robin Hood, The Thief of Baghdad* and *The Black Pirate,* consolidating himself as a major star — and with the earnings to match. Pickfair, the Fairbanks/Pickford home was legendary for its Hollywood opulence.

Such was the power of the movies to attract large audiences, and therefore large amounts of money, that Hollywood underwent its very own inflationary spiral; by 1926, Gloria Swanson was being offered $400,000, plus 50 per cent of the profits, to make just three pictures a year. This was because Swanson was a star. The star system grew up in the 1920s amid an atmosphere bursting with expectancy. By the time the talkies arrived in 1927, more than 57 million people per year were regularly going to the movies. Being able to reach this number of people had extraordinary effects on the mass psyche. Even in the early 1920s when audiences had not reached anything like this volume, one Rodolpho Alfonzo Rafaelo Pierre Filibert Guglielmi di Valentina d'Antoguolla, commonly known as Rudolph Valentino, caused a sensation. His appearance in *The Sheik* (1921) consolidated his reputation as a heart-throb. This status was borne out by the fact that, upon his sudden death at the age of 31 in 1926, thousands of women took

● **OPPOSITE** Poster for Fritz Lang's *Metropolis,* 1926. Showing the German Expressionist influence in its graphics and the inspiration of New York in the cityscape.

● **ABOVE** Rudolph Valentino. Heartthrob and testament to the power of the movies.

● **LEFT** Two women mourning the death of their idol. More than 15,000 women packed Broadway trying to view the body of Valentino as it lay in state in 1926.

to the veil and followed his coffin through the streets (several fanatics even committed suicide); they were mourning the loss, not of a man, but of a romantic image. They had only really known him in black and white on the big screen, but it was enough to inspire undying devotion.

This kind of phenomenon was also enough to convince the film companies that vertical integration was the way forward. For this reason, when the talkies first began to make their impact felt, the major film companies began to open their own chains of movie theatres. This paved the way for a new and popularly experienced form of fantasy architecture, of the type seen in Grauman's Chinese Theater in Los Angeles or in the suburban movie theatres in England. Furthermore the building programme instigated by the movie makers was accompanied by a massive hike in admission charges (in the United States, from 50¢ to $1.65), but this increase did nothing to deter the crowds and ensured an even better return on the investment of the movie moguls. In any case, a night at the movies was seen to be a good value – with cartoons, a serial, a 'B' movie and the main feature,

● **BELOW** Gary Cooper in an early performance, screened in what appears to be a railway carriage.

● **BOTTOM** Interior of the New Victoria, London, 1930. Predominantly Egyptian motifs were employed in the decoration of this movie house. The massive cinema organ pipes can just be seen on the right of the illustration.

perhaps interspersed by community singing or a recital on the cinema organ.

By the 1930s, three New York City boroughs – Manhattan, Brooklyn and the Bronx – had 83 movie theatres between them all, all of which seated 2,000 or more people. In addition to this there were 16 other theatres with 3,000-plus capacity and, finally, the mighty Gaumont Palace, which held 6,200 souls in one auditorium. The advent of the talkies in 1927 had much to do with this explosion. After Al Jolson, already a big recording and radio star, had sung a short song he uttered the immortal line, 'Wait a minute, wait a minute . . . you ain't seen nothing yet'. The film was *The Jazz Singer* and its 1927 release heralded the start of the movies as really big business.

In retrospect, the birth of the talking picture was extraordinarily well timed. Hollywood took on the principles of sound for pictures in advance of the Wall Street Crash of 1929, and consequently there were backers available to finance the change. The success of the talkies meant that much of the money borrowed by the studios to finance this development had been paid back by the time of the crash. Furthermore, in the ensuing years of the Depression, people turned towards the movies as an escape route, a fantasy world at a far remove from the grim realities of everyday life. It is not surprising, therefore, that the combination of sound on film and the Depression should give rise to one of the most fantasy-inspired genres of all, the Hollywood musical. The popularity of this form of film was capitalized upon by the industry and was undoubtedly partially responsible for the rise in attendances at movie theatres.

After the introduction of sound in 1927, audience figures rose from the aforementioned 57 million to over 90 million in 1930. This growth in audiences is commensurate with the increase in theatres equipped for sound. In 1929 there were only 9,000 such theatres, but two years later there were over 13,000. The increase in popularity of the movies was instrumental in furthering the careers of many actors, singers and dancers, from Fred Astaire and Ginger Rogers, to Bing Crosby, Bette Davis, James Cagney, Katharine Hepburn, Cary Grant, Joan Crawford and countless others. Film was and remained an inspiration for many people, while reflecting an innate ability to comment on the state of the nation – and sometimes the world, as in the work of Lubitsch.

However, even when in a lighter vein, the movies were seen to entertain as well as represent

a distillation of common feeling. The 'Gold Diggers' series of films was one such case. Perhaps the most famous of this series of films produced in Hollywood from the late 1920s onward is *Gold Diggers of 1933*, which featured the song 'We're in the Money', in which the line 'old man depression you are through you done us wrong' was sung while a line of girls twirled huge silver-dollar pieces. The antithesis of this song was 'My Forgotten Man'; in that number, men were seen 'marching . . . marching . . . always marching'. The question remains: was the song an allegory for the Depression or a plea for a lost love? With the faint tang of paranoia surrounding the issue of Communism in the United States at this time, it is unlikely that the song was in any way a criticism of the American economy or that nation's treatment of its unemployed. This film also marked the flowering of the talent of Busby Berkeley, whose fame for symmetrical dance routines — imaginatively set, choreographed and photographed — became a visual trademark for

● **ABOVE** Publicity poster for James Cagney in *Public Enemy*.
The 1930s saw a wholesale use of the Prohibition years of the 1920s as subject matter, as the studios promoted the likes of Edward G Robinson, George Raft and Cagney to superstar status in their portrayals of gangsters.

● **LEFT** Young Joan Crawford, depicted against a strikingly modernistic backdrop.

many of the films of this era.

Tie-ins between film, music and radio were many, with screen stars often doubling as recording artists (to this end, radio studios were built in Burbank, near Hollywood). Thus the films served to promote the recordings, and vice versa. Fred Astaire, for instance, issued many records on which he was featured dancing, the noise of his taps recorded against an orchestral backing! However, 'Top Hat', 'Flying Down to Rio', 'Change Partners', 'Night and Day' and other songs, all successful in their own right, because of the movies came to be inextricably linked to Astaire, clearly demonstrating the power of this medium when backed up by records and the ubiquitous radio.

Entertainment in the 1920s and 1930s was char-

acterized not only by a certain stylistic content which we immediately associate with the Jazz Age, but it was also very much the result of technological innovation and application. At this time the Technicolor process was first developed and used to its best effect, in films like Walt Disney's *Snow White* (1937). *The Wizard of Oz* (1939) also put this process to good use – in the scene in which humdrum black and white became dazzling Technicolor after Dorothy had made her journey, via tornado into the Land of Oz.

The growth of mass entertainment represented a huge and permanent change in the way in which people expected to be diverted on their evenings out. Used as we are today to the idea of mega-entertainment, with audiences experiencing events

● **LEFT** The tableau climaxing 'By a Waterfall', from *Footlight Parade*, 1933. This is a characteristic Busby Berkeley set piece: dozens of beautiful girls in symmetrical splendour, entertaining the masses with a grandeur which was in direct opposition to the grim realities of the age.

●**ABOVE** Publicity poster for *The Wizard of Oz*, 1939, Metro-Goldwyn-Mayer's Technicolor triumph.

●**RIGHT** Publicity poster for Alex Korda's *Things to Come*, 1936.

● **ABOVE** Wurlitzer 950,
Paul Fuller, 1939.
The jukebox-as-architecture
in what was perhaps its most
gaudy incarnation. The
nickelodeon proved to be a
primary tool in the success
and growth of the American
record industry in the 1930s,
with the juke-joint becoming
an indispensible part of
many towns across the
nation.

simultaneously around the world, the magnitude of
the relatively new experience for nearly a million
people – of buying the same record, seeing the
same film nationwide or listening to the same dance
band on a national network – can easily escape us
today. There are countless examples of the effect
of the movies on national behaviour. When Clark
Gable did not wear a vest in *It Happened One
Night,* a nation's men reputedly shed their under-
garments. Veronica Lake sported her peek-a-boo
hair and a new style of coiffure was born. Men
wanted to learn to sing like Bing Crosby, so Crosby
recorded an instructive song 'Learn to Croon'.
Clara Bow starred as the 'It' girl in the eponymous
film, and the Hays Office was born to guard the
nation's morals: Clearly, the impact of mass entertainment was on more than an ephemeral level. It
influenced the very way in which the countries of
the world moved, thought, dressed, acted and
perceived their very own lives. From King Vidor's
The Crowd of 1928 to the British production of Alex
Korda's futuristic *Things to Come* in 1936, the movies
demonstrated themselves as one arm of what was
a studiedly modern and innovative industry.

Mass entertainment covered the home, the
movies and the bar-rooms of the United States. By
the end of the 1930s the jukebox had arrived, soon
occupying pride of place in countless diners and
bars. At this time these mechanized music boxes,
these miniatures of modern architecture, accounted
for the consumption of 30 million records per year.
Big business was growing around the entertainment industry as more and more people became
caught up in the search for entertainment. Money
in the shape of the wealthy Rockefellers developed
interests in the world of entertainment, with Manhattan's glittering Radio City Music Hall part of the
Rockefeller Center complex built by that old-money
New York family. Meanwhile, Metro-Goldwyn-
Mayer, RKO, Twentieth Century-Fox, Columbia
and Paramount studios came to dominate the movie
industry.

By the 1930s, the previous decade came to be
known as the Jazz Age, an epithet deriving from
the novel and exciting musical genre. Jazz was
indeed 'new' music to the predominantly white
classes, who threw caution to the wind during the
Prohibition years of the 1920s and enjoyed the syn-
copation and exuberance of jazz music. Paul White-
man, the self-styled 'King of Jazz', played frequently
at the Coconut Grove in New York, which itself was
a manifestation of yet another form of entertainment peculiar to this era, the nightclub.

The nightclub was a legitimate offspring of the
speakeasy, which had grown up when social drink-
ing went underground after the introduction of the
Prohibition law in January 1920. This constitutional
amendment, which banned the consumption of

●**BELOW** Rockefeller Center, New York, with RCA Building; statue of Prometheus in foreground (by Paul Manship, 1930).

alcohol, resulted in two major occurrences: the gang warfare in Chicago, with Al Capone at the head of an immense bootlegging empire, and the election of Franklin Delano Roosevelt in 1932, on a ticket promising the repeal of the Prohibition act. During the 12 years in which the ban was in force, the nightclub grew up. It subsequently emerged in the 1920s and 1930s as *the* fashionable place to be seen, the haunt of the beau monde.

Nightclubs like the famous Cotton Club in New York's Harlem operated a system of racial segre-

gation, wherein the only way a black man or woman could get into the place was as an entertainer or waiter. Nevertheless, the Cotton Club saw such greats as Duke Ellington and Lena Horne grace its stage, bringing great wit and intelligence to a musical form which in the 1920s had been dubbed 'the devil's music'. It had been so named by a less enlightened minority, a group which had no hope of seeing it as an art form greatly contributing to the atmosphere of change, progress and modernity permeating this extraordinary era.

Chaise longue in plywood, Marcel Breuer for Isokon, 1935.

CHAPTER FOUR

MODERNISM AND THE INTERNATIONAL STYLE

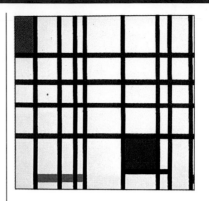

Modernism was more than just a stylistic nuance of the 1920s and 1930s. It was, in its fullest sense, the merging of various strands of development in art, architecture and design which had been in existence since before World War I.

The De Stijl movement in Holland, the designs of Le Corbusier and, later, the work of the Bauhaus all helped to create the essence of what has commonly been called the 'Modern Movement'.

However, far from being a unified 'movement' in the true sense of the word, the architects and designers who were to produce the forms commonly recognized as Modernist were individuals. Although they were open to influence from each other and shared many common utopian ideas, the sense of there being a cohesive movement with a set of declared aims was to a large extent missing. Even the bringing together of modern architects in 1928 (under the banner of the *Congrès Internationaux d'Architecture Moderne*), in order to promote internationalism in architecture, failed to cement a lasting bond.

The common ground of the so-called Modern Movement was therefore to be found in the materials used, and perhaps more importantly the way in which those materials were used. For the first time, materials such as glass, reinforced concrete and tubular steel gained general currency and formed the basis of a new architectural and design style. It was the properties of these substances which contributed in a large way to the forms which characterize this particular area of 1920s and 1930s style.

Modernist icons such as Marcel Breuer's 'Wassily Chair', designed in 1925 at the Bauhaus, owe their form not only to the vision of the designer, but to the properties of the materials from which they were made. The strength of tubular steel allowed

● **ABOVE** *Composition with Red, Yellow and Blue*, Piet Mondrian, 1937–42.
The work of the De Stijl movement was characterized by a use of primary colours and a strong reliance on the supposed 'purity' of the horizontal and vertical, as seen in this work by Piet Mondrian.

● **LEFT** 'Wassily Chair', Marcel Breuer, 1925.

● **OPPOSITE** Student Apartment Block, Dessau Bauhaus, Walter Gropius, 1925.
Architecture displaying all the traits of Modernism in design materials and execution.

for a lightweight design with flat leather surfaces intersecting to make an innovatory and comfortable armchair. The fact that Breuer named the chair after the Russian Constructivist painter, Wassily Kandinsky, hints at the interaction between those at the cutting edge of art and design at this time. Indeed, Constructivist art reveals its influence in the intersection of the flat leather surfaces of the Wassily chair.

Plastics, too, made their impact at this time. These new synthetics found an interface with Modernism in their use by, among others, Serge Chermayeff (b.1900) and Wells Coates (1895–1958) in Britain, notably in their designs for radio housings in the 1930s. Coates, like the Russian-born Chermayeff, was an architect, and the fact that architects were

designing domestic objects intended for mass-distribution helped to introduce the ideas of modernity into the lives of ordinary people. Technology was seen to enter the home on a grand scale, and what is more it came in a cabinet which expressed modernity in its look as well as its contents.

In terms of architecture and some designs for the home, it is the absence of ornament and dominance of the straight line which characterize this arm of 1920s and 1930s style. Although aesthetically appealing to some modern eyes, many of the Modernist buildings, when first constructed, were intended to appear as radical departures from the norm. In previous decades architecture for the masses had been derived from the cheapest application possible of traditional house-building techniques. Modernism sought to break away from this pattern and answer the need for housing by employing mass-production techniques to the con-

struction of housing. Therefore, for economic as well as aesthetic reasons, the walls, windows, drainage systems and some interior parts of Modernist architecture were prefabricated. Externally at least, the use of reinforced concrete in prefabricated sections served to create a look which was nothing if not minimalist.

In 1927 Ludwig Mies van der Rohe (1886–1969) was instrumental in bringing together the designs of modern architects for workers' housing in one project, the *Weissenhof Siedlung.* In an area of parkland overlooking the city of Stuttgart (today in West Germany), the work of Modernist architects such as Walter Gropius, Mart Stam, Le Corbusier, Peter Behrens and Mies himself was brought together to demonstrate modern solutions to the problem of creating cheap housing for workers. It is this utopian vision, expressed in many of the buildings at the *Siedlung,* which was the driving force

● **TOP** Ekco Model AD36 wireless, Wells Coates, 1935.

● **ABOVE** Tea service, Margaret Heymann-Löbenstein, 1930.
Trained at the Bauhaus from 1919 to 1922, Löbenstein's design has a Modernist 'machine' aesthetic about it, while obviously displaying the marks of craft production techniques. The marriage of the two was among the aims of the early Bauhaus.

behind what can loosely be called the Modern Movement. It was the nearest anyone ever came to a cogent statement of what Modernism was initially about.

These buildings were characterized by the use of flat roofs and standardized parts, white-painted walls and rectilinear geometry, and as such did much to crystallize a new, Modernist style – devoid of homage to what were seen as the overornamented styles of previous decades. Elements of this rationalist stance can be found in the designs of many other self-professed Modernists, who designed furniture and lighting as well as the buildings in which to put them.

The consolidation of the Communist regime, together with the growth of National Socialism in Germany during the late 1920s and 1930s, served to catalyze the spread of Modernism to England and the United States, with the emigration of men and women who can be seen as the prime movers in the world of Modernist design. Kandinsky, El Lissitzky and Chermayeff all left Russia for Germany. From there, Chermayeff, together with Gropius, Erich Mendelsohn, Breuer and later Mies van der Rohe, made the trip to England and then to the United States. Walter Gropius, the erstwhile director of the Bauhaus, was invited to teach in Chicago by Philip Johnson. So it can be seen that both the birth and the spread of Modernism were aided by the spread of extremist politics.

However, this migration did not occur largely until after Hitler had gained full power in 1933. Up to this time, Modernism was employed in the con-struction of housing for ordinary people – but never on the kind of utopian scale which its progenitors had hoped for. There were, however, some examples of the successful use of rationalist principles in the construction of housing. Walter Gropius's Siemensstadt development in Berlin (1929–30) was one of them. At about the same time (1930) Karl Ehn, the city architect of Vienna, designed the Karl Marx Hof with his team. These estates became places of pilgrimage for designers and architects alike, who wished to see the precepts of Modernism put into pratice.

Modernism itself was in transition from its role as an architectural phenomenon born of sincere utopianism into that of an acceptably modern fashion. An exhibition held in New York in 1931–32, under the aegis of the Museum of Modern Art, was designed to bring the fact of the existence of Modernism to a wider audience. In the catalogue accompanying the exhibition, coauthors Henry-Russell Hitchcock and Philip Johnson coined the phrase 'The International Style'. According to Hitchcock and Johnson, buildings in the International Style were to follow precise aesthetic and construction principles – the conception of architectural space as volume (as opposed to mass, regularity and flexibility) and the technically perfect use of materials. The influence of one Charles-Edouard Jeanneret, commonly known as Le Corbusier, becomes important in that the International Style is characterized by attempts by the architects involved to induce the ideas of weightlessness in buildings by the use of cantilevered extensions. Through

● **BELOW** Empire State
Building, New York, Shreve,
Lamb and Harmon,
1929–31.
Skyscraper style as opposed
to International Style, but
nonetheless modern in
construction.

cantilevering, load-bearing elements of the building
are shifted back into the interior, thus allowing for
the construction of light spaces lit by what appear
to be walls of glass.

Curiously enough, Hitchcock and Johnson railed
against the skyscraper, which must be seen as the
logical roof of Modernist building methods. Although first built in the 19th century, skyscrapers
were at that time becoming more and more common, particularly in New York, with the construction
of the Chrysler, General Electric and Empire State
buildings, all dating from the 1930s in the post-
International Style era. Johnson and Hitchcock
identified that a building in the International Style
should be constructed of steel, glass and reinforced
concrete and should have a geometrically derived
and organized appearance. Their mistrust of the
skyscraper was derived from the ornamentation
applied to buildings with rationalist construction at

● **LEFT** Chrysler Building spire by night, New York, William van Alen, 1928–30. Viewed from the Empire State Building, the Chrysler spire proclaims the style and importance of the Chrysler Corporation in no uncertain terms. Once more this type of building could only be executed through the utilization of the most modern building and engineering techniques.

● **ABOVE** De La Warr Pavilion, Bexhill-on-Sea, Mendelsohn & Chermayeff, 1935–36.
Showing the elevation which looks towards the sea, the use of cantilevering, concrete, standardized windows and rails can clearly be seen. It is a Modernist building in design and function.

● **RIGHT** Fagus Shoe Factory, Alfeld an der Leine, Walter Gropius, 1911.
A truly proto-Modernist building, the Fagus factory was among the first to incorporate glass curtain walling into its design. The load-bearing elements in the frame of the building made this possible.

their heart.

Geometry, steel, glass and reinforced concrete are of course classic Modernist materials and their employment is a distinctively Modernist device, found as early as 1911 in Walter Gropius's Fagus Shoe Factory, in Alfeld.

However, the International Style had gained credence in architectural circles long before it was named by Johnson and Hitchcock. Indeed, it is difficult to decide whether there was a true International Style or whether Modernism evolved into a style which could be so-named. Its very modernity owed little to regional and national styles of architecture and so was able to transcend geographical boundaries. This, at least, is the argument which was propounded by Hitchcock and Johnson, but in all, the International Style was a purely superficial attempt to give a collective name to an architecture which could encompass buildings as different in conception and construction as Gerrit Rietveld's Schröder House in Utrecht (1924) and the De La Warr Pavilion in Bexhill (1935–36).

There are obvious stylistic links between many buildings which employ Modernist construction techniques and yet are the result of either the injection of private capital, as in Le Corbusier's *Maisons Blanches* or the direction of status-seeking local councils with a sympathetic Modernist bent. For instance, Mendelsohn and Chermayeff built the De

La Warr Pavilion in Bexhill, Sussex in 1935. It used the principles of cantilevering and the glass wall, and was obviously both a Modernist building and in the International Style. Likewise, Maxwell Fry's Sun House, built in Hampstead, London, in 1936, shared many of the qualities of Le Corbusier's Villa Stein (1926) at Garches, France, with its terraces, rectilinearity and skilfull juggling of masses and voids, creating the lightness and modernity concomitant with the new modern architecture.

The *Maison Blanche* had spread to England with Marcel Breuer's 'New Ways', which was built in Northampton in 1926. But after World War II the precepts of Modernism were to affect the look of buildings in far more than the wealthy private sector, which could afford to pay for the likes of Behrens and Le Corbusier to build modern villas for a fashionable clientele. Clearly, Modernism can be seen as a true style of the 1920s and 1930s, in that it found its greatest and most widespread acceptance after it had been transformed from avantgarde to newly fashionable by the likes of Johnson and Hitchcock. Indeed, the vogue for the Moderne continued from the mid-1920s to the outbreak of World War II.

● **ABOVE** The Schröder House, Utrecht, Gerrit Rietveld, 1923–24. Often quoted as a Modernist icon because of its geometric composition and white walls, the Schröder House is a combination of steel frame, wood and traditional brick construction, with concrete used for balconies and awnings.

Radiator grille by Jacques Delamarre, 1929; from the Chanin Building, New York.

CHAPTER FIVE

ART DECO: A STYLE FOR TWO DECADES

Art Deco was a style spanning not only the 1920s and 1930s, but also a broad range of different areas and objects – from architecture to interior design, from ceramics to furniture, from textiles to graphics, and beyond.

As a recognizable, crystallized style, it has its origins in the highly decorative pieces that could be found in the *Exposition des Arts Décoratifs et Industriels Modernes,* held in Paris in 1925 (the exhibition from which the style also derived its name).

It would be a mistake, however, to assume that there is a definite 'starting point' for Art Deco. Rather, there was a gradual shift among designers and architects, at first in France and later all over the world, towards certain sources of inspiration for mostly applied decoration to buildings and interiors, as well as for furniture, ceramics, glass and even plastics. Although the Art Deco label was used to describe certain types of furniture after 1925 – largely because of the Paris exhibition – the techniques of production, together with some of the forms which are now thought of as characterizing Art Deco, had in fact been in evidence since before World War I, particularly in France.

Art Deco started its life as a 'high style' and ended it as arguably the most populist and perhaps *the* most popular of all recognizable post-World War I styles. Ultimately, the style fed upon itself. At its most mundane, it became further and further removed from its origins in the decorative arts, especially with the (over) use, distillation and repetition of its most durable decorative motifs, such as the fan, chevron and ziggurat.

At its most opulent, Art Deco is distinguished by

●**BELOW** Six Asprey dining chairs and chromed-metal table inlaid with Lalique glass panels, 1920s.
One strain of high Art Deco, produced for a wealthy and discerning clientele.

a lavish use of largely added decoration. In furniture this could take the form of veneers of exotic woods, inlays of mother-of-pearl, snakeskin or sharkskin coverings, layers of Oriental lacquer, or applied-bronze mounts. The work of the Parisian cabinetmaker Emile-Jacques Ruhlmann (1879–1933) is highly indicative of the extravagant and luxurious end of Art Deco craftsmanship in the 1920s and 1930s.

Ruhlmann occupied a prominent – and popular – pavilion at the 1925 Paris exhibition, but even some years subsequent to this, the Ruhlmann marque came to signify first and foremost luxury, but luxury which could be produced in the newly fashionable modern style. Under the guidance of Ruhlmann himself, Ruhlmann's company was in effect continuing the tradition of French luxury-goods production, dating back to the royal patronage of the 18th century. It is perhaps due to Ruhlmann's ability to respond to the tastes of a wealthy, discerning clientele, that the output of his workshops came to be synonymous with top-quality Art Deco furniture.

In architecture, especially in North America, the detailing on the outside of buildings would often contain the characteristic fan shapes, flowers, and other stylized elements so often connected with Art Deco. In interior design, typical Art Deco spaces

● **LEFT** Gold mask from the tomb of Tutankhamun, *c*1340 BC.
The discovery of the Egyptian Pharaoh's tomb in 1922 provided Art Deco designers with a rich source of ornate motifs.

● **BELOW** Table watch with Egyptian scarab wing sides, *c*1925.
The timepiece illustrates the use of ancient forms from Egypt, and their adoption as 'modern' at around the time of the 1925 Paris Exposition.

58

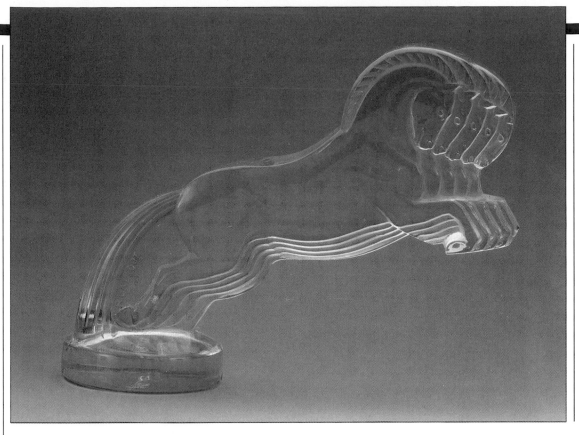

● **LEFT** *Cinq Chevaux* car mascot, René Lalique, 1920s. Luxury on a car bonnet is illustrated by this Lalique glass sculpture. Designed to be lit from underneath, it would have put the finishing touch on a Bugatti.

would often be marked by their use of panelling in coloured glass, mirrors or lacquerwork. Later, synthetic materials such as Vitrolite or Lucite would be used to gain similar effects in a more Modern idiom.

In the main, the recurring motifs employed by American architects in the decoration of Art Deco buildings were broadly derived from Egyptian, Meso-American and other exotic sources. The tomb of Tutankhamen had been discovered near Luxor in 1922 and the subsequent publicity had both offered designers a new source of inspiration and paved the way for public acceptance of ancient – but newly fashionable – motifs.

The reliance on the straight line, lightning bolt and often-layered geometry of much later Art Deco sometimes has been linked to Cubist techniques of representation developed by Braque and Picasso, which predate the 1925 Paris Exposition by at least a decade. But while it is a relatively easy task to find an echo of this artistic style in some Art Deco design, there is no real need to forge a connection between what are essentially unrelated, though contemporaneous, phenomena.

However, related strains of design can be found in the 1920s and '30s which are loosely categorized under the blanket term of Art Deco. But there is a difference between what could be termed 'high Art Deco', comprising objects produced by the likes of Ruhlmann, Jean Dunand, René Lalique and Jean Puiforcat, and the concurrent fashion for the 'Moderne'. This was a style which was to borrow quite heavily from the visual repertoire of Parisian Art Deco in the quest for fashionability.

The phenomenon of the Moderne is usually considered distinct from that of high Art Deco; thus the latter term should not be used to describe the bentwood tables and chairs designed for the British Isokon Furniture Company by Marcel Breuer (1902–81) in the 1930s, or even the more Moderne items created by Irish-born Eileen Gray (1878–1976), a Paris-based designer. Both Gray and Breuer, as examples, are strongly associated with 1920s and 1930s design and hence, almost automatically, Art Deco. But Gray's impetus to design sprang from an almost Modernist bent, and on the whole she sought to avoid historical motifs for decorative inspiration (except in her earlier lacquered pieces). Likewise, Marcel Breuer, leading light of the Bauhaus and chair designer *extraordinaire,* was an affirmed Modernist and designed from a politically informed position with the utopian fervour characterizing the so-called 'Modern Movement'.

Clearly, neither of these two designers' Modernist works should be associated with high-style Parisian Art Deco, but, as will be seen, there are many grey areas in 1920s and 1930s style, where ostensibly different areas of design and different stylistic categories overlap. It is perhaps this fact which contributes to the creation of a recognizable, multi-faceted 1920s and 1930s style.

Not surprisingly, 'high' Art Deco is more concerned with expensive, luxurious objects with high production values, and costs made not for the masses but for a fashionable and discerning clientele. The underlit mascots designed in glass for car radiators by René Lalique (1860–1945) were

● **ABOVE** Three figures in silver and bronze, on marble bases, 1920.
The figure on the far right is by the sculptor Chiparus.

obviously not intended to sit upon the Ford Model 'T'. These Lalique figures represent yet another arm of Art Deco production, that of mass-produced decorative sculpture. The sylph-like bronze nudes bearing aloft glass globes and the elaborate chryselephantine figures gamboling with gay abandon are today synonymous with Art Deco. Yet in truth they represent a departure from, rather than an integral part of, the style. In essence, many of these sculptures are far too naturalistic to be included in the more stylized canon of Art Deco artefacts. Nevertheless, they do represent certain elements of the obsessions with health, sport, naturalism and the erotic female form that marked the 1920s and 1930s.

In the United States, and to a lesser extent in Great Britain, the Art Deco style was taken to heart by designers and the public alike. The entrance halls of corporate buildings, particularly in Manhattan, were often decorated in the Art Deco style and for the people of New York at least, a certain shining era in the history of the city is symbolized by these Art Deco interiors.

That these motifs originally associated with high Art Deco pieces eventually found their way – in however a stylized and distilled form – into the more public domain, for example, Radio City Music Hall in New York or the Odeon Cinema in London's Leicester Square, is a testament to both the power of fashion and the lure of the new in the 1920s and 1930s. Indeed, such cinema designs probably greatly assisted in the dissemination of the stylistic language which has come to be known as Art Deco.

Today, Art Deco has become something of a blanket term for objects and decorations which contain recognizable motifs of the original style, however faithful or ersatz. When the bulk of what is now known as Art Deco was produced during the 1920s and 1930s, it undoubtedly displayed some of the surface traits of 'high Art Deco', but lacked the luxuriance, singularity and investment of design and labour which resulted in the glass creations of Lalique, the exquisite silver of Jean Puiforcat, or the precious jewellery sold by Van Cleef and Arpels, Tiffany and Cartier.

Art Deco moved from the arena of high fashion into the workaday world, bringing with it the values and the looks associated with high living, a fat bank balance and an opulence which could be set against the world's economic depression. The spread of the style has been described as a reaction to the austerity and deprivation occasioned by World War I; if this is the case, then it is not surprising to find the echo of the luxury of the Art Deco motif in places of public entertainment as well as in the sun-ray gates, front doors and windows of the British suburban semi-detached house. At its most popular level, Art Deco was a symbol for a new postwar age, an age which was able to outlive the economic and political upheavals still to come. The style could only achieve this by being assimilated into a broader and more pupular aesthetic, a process which was aided and encouraged in many different ways.

In terms of architecture there are further notable examples of Art Deco forms which found their way

into corporate buildings and therefore into common currency. In England, the ribbon development of the Great West Road allowed for the construction of the Hoover factory. A huge Art Deco-like edifice – designed by Wallis, Gilbert & Partners and constructed in 1933 – the Hoover factory also bears some Modernist traits in its design. Indeed, the Hoover building symbolizes the strength Art Deco motifs must have had in conveying the modernity and *esprit nouveau* of the interwar years.

● **ABOVE** Crystal glasses and decanter, possibly by Baccarat.
Once again this type of object represents the high Art Deco from which more populist copies of and variations on the style derived.

● **LEFT** The Hoover Factory, London, Wallis, Gilbert and Partners, 1933.
Art Deco and Egyptian motifs were used in this building to signify the modernity of the Hoover Corporation to the public. The building stands today as a monument to the popular segment of Art Deco design.

Likewise, Manhattan's Chrysler Building, designed by William van Alen and constructed between 1928 and 1930, used a steel cladding technique at its pinnacle, both to assist in differentiating it from the other skyscrapers beginning to dominate the New York skyline and to speak to New York — and maybe even the world? — of modernity, fashion and style. The decoration on the top of this building comprises a telescoped semicircle repeated four times and diminishing in size as it brings the building to a point. Each semicircle has inset triangular apertures, the lower ones of which are glazed. The impact of a metal-topped building in the middle of New York, especially when it was caught by sunlight or lit up at night, was intended to be seen as a modern symbol; at the same time, the corporate image of Chrysler would of course benefit. Once again a building was seen to evoke the modern spirit of a new age in its applied decoration, and although it is doubtful that the term was used in direct connection with the Chrysler Building, an *esprit nouveau* was definitely in the air on both sides of the Atlantic between the two world wars. This Art Deco-derived decoration was not seen as historicist — it was modern, fashionable and undeniably of its time, a powerful and omni-present symbol of a new era which ostensibly owed nothing to the decades, indeed the centuries, before it.

The use of the words *esprit nouveau* brings in once again the 1925 Paris exhibition and the work of Le Corbusier (1887–1965), whose pavilion at the fair was called *L'Esprit Nouveau.* The term serves to highlight both the difference and the meeting point between Art Deco and other forms of design considered modern, or Moderne, during the 1920s and 1930s. The Paris Exposition, which was supposed to be a forum for the display of the decorative arts, contained the aforementioned pavilion designed by the Swiss-born architect — an exhibit which flew in the face of the intended spirit of the exhibition and yet promoted a bolder, more uncompromising approach to design, whose key was the maxim that modern decorative art 'had no decor'. The objects with which Le Corbusier furnished his pavilion were what he referred to as 'typical forms'. It contained office furniture by Roneo, bentwood chairs by Thonet Brothers and sculpture by Jacques Lipchitz. Some cubist paintings adorned the walls. The space was completed by a model aeroplane and some rugs on the floor.

The forms found in Le Corbusier's *Pavillon de L'Esprit Nouveau* can in no way be described as high-style Art Deco, yet they were to be seen by fairgoers alongside the works of Ruhlmann, Lalique et al. In a way, the appearance of these things together represents the ferment of design theory and practice which went into the formation of the recognizable phenomenon known as 1920s and '30s style. It is worth remembering, however, that Art Deco, either the high-style or more distilled, populist variety, was not the only element of the multifaceted style marking these two decades.

Carpet, Karl Maes, 1930s.

CHAPTER SIX

THE MODERNE:
COMMERCIAL APPLICATIONS
IN EUROPE AND
THE UNITED STATES

When the 1920s and 1930s are discussed in terms of their style, there is an immediate, almost inevitable slant towards the term 'Art Deco'. The fashionable liking for objects produced in the 1920s and '30s, which has continued since the mid-1970s, has led to the blanket description of art objects and consumer goods displaying some of the geometric hallmarks of interwar styling as Art Deco. Dealers in 'antiques' thus find that, by use of this description, prices can be automatically increased and the unwary or unknowing buyer is often gulled into purchasing an everyday object displaying just some vestigial traces of the 'Deco' style. The truth is that often the objects offered as legitimate 'Art Deco' today were conceived in the 1920s and 1930s as Art Moderne, 'Moderne', modernistic or just plain modern or contemporary. These terms cover the hybrid objects which have as part of their construction and decoration Art Deco motifs, streamform styling and modernistic geometrical configurations and decoration. Art Deco is therefore merely one component of the stylistic language of the Moderne and has been used, albeit as a misnomer, for many objects of the era.

Moderne, modernistic and Art Moderne are therefore more or less interchangeable terms for a design idiom which could be found in situations as diverse as interior design, furniture, architecture, glass, ceramics and set designs for both film and stage. The Moderne represented that fusion of contemporary styles from various disciplines and, although originally conceived as a highly fashionable design style, it soon permeated society, through the medium of film and through the plethora of popular, readily available goods – from vacuum cleaners to chinaware – on sale in Woolworth and department stores everywhere.

The modernity inherent in the everyday object, such as a radio or other electrical appliance, often brought this modern idiom directly into the homes of the ordinary person, but often it would have to have existed alongside objects from the previous century, or at the very least the accumulation of various furniture and effects which every home enjoys. It is perhaps this incongruity with its ordinary surroundings which was to militate against the success of the Moderne in the ordinary home and, conversely, herald its application and success in the public domain – in hotels, cocktail bars, shops, film sets and even the interiors of ocean liners. These interiors were conceived as part of a total modernizing process which created within the confines of

● **BELOW** Bizarre 'Inspiration' plate, coffee set and vase, Clarice Cliff for A Wilkinson Ltd, 1930s. The coffee set is of most interest as a piece of Moderne design. Its geometry is more 'naturalized', the floral motif softening the angularity of the design.

● **ABOVE** Chairs, Le Corbusier, 1920s.
Made from chromed steel and upholstered in ponyskin, these chairs border on the Moderne because of the quality and expense of the materials used.

the foyer or dining salon the complete Moderne setting. This was the case both in Europe and the United States.

By 1926, many American manufacturers were producing goods in the Art Moderne or Modernist style, which in many cases meant the application of masses of zigzags and triangles in an attempt to recreate the styles seen at the Paris Exposition the previous year. Furnishing fabrics displaying these Art Deco-derived motifs were used to upholster furniture which was fundamentally no different in shape from the furniture produced for the mass market two to three years before. Not surprisingly, at this stage in its development, the Moderne failed to do particularly good business in the domestic market and, worse, it was viewed as 'pastiche' by commentators on home décor. It was not until the widespread use of tubular steel in furniture design that the Moderne found its true métier; at that point the novel material was seen to move 'from the operating theatre into the cocktail bar'.

Teamed with either modernistic fabric designs or plain leather for upholstery, and with chrome-plated tubular steel, the utilitarian, strictly Modernist (opposed to all the other terms) origins were forgotten and a new style of luxury furniture was born. Le Corbusier's *Grand Confort* seating of 1928 was just such a luxury item. Although the rational Mod-

ernist background of Le Corbusier's designs are not in question here, such was the nature of much of his patronage (that is, wealthy clients) that the austerity reserved for his projects for workers' housing, or for a less luxurious chair in steel tubing and canvas, was not so much placed to one side as melded with the qualities associated with soft leather and overstuffed comfortable armchairs. Therefore the qualities of the Moderne were allowed to come to the fore – there was a union between a 'seriously' derived design idiom and those qualities engendered by the lure of commercialism and the touch of luxury. However, this is not to say that design realized in the style of the Moderne or Art Moderne was not design seriously thought about and executed.

The work of Le Corbusier, in whichever medium, has a gravity about it arising from the intellectual justification for his work which he strove so hard to impart. The fact that some of his designs have the signs of an investment of labour, and hence luxury, about them does not mean that they were conceived outside of the strict Modernist tenets Le Corbusier had delineated. Likewise, other designers were not just 'cribbing' from the new lexicon of modern styling, but in bringing together certain materials and techniques they were creating a style for an age.

67

One such designer was Eileen Gray. Her designs were the result of an attempt not to repeat the decorative nuances of a past age, but, rather, to attempt to key into the modern values associated with materials like tubular steel, and furthermore to find modern resonances in strong geometric compositions. Having lived in Paris from 1902, Gray began her career as a designer studying techniques of Japanese lacquering, an art truly reserved for the luxury end of the market. By the 1920s, however, she had begun to fuse the functional aesthetic of Breueresque/Corbusian furniture design with a sense of luxury realized in her use of traditional cabinet-making materials like walnut, kingwood and polished brass. In this way Eileen Gray combined the tradition of Ruhlmann with the contemporaneousness of the Modern Movement, drawing from the stark utopianism of Modernism a design sensibility well attuned to the fashionable *Parisienne*'s desire for contemporaneity, good taste and the one-off design. In the mid-to late 1920s Gray went one step further towards the total joining of Modernism and luxury when she built her and Jean Badovici's house, E.1027, in the south of France. It was a starkly Modernist villa, filled with her furniture, rugs and designs and representing the perfect marriage of austerity and luxury.

The Moderne was brought to a far wider audience through the medium of film, with sets, found in films coming out of the MGM studios, often designed by Cedric Gibbons (who also designed the Oscar statuette). Sets would become wildly lux-

● **ABOVE** Armchair in tubular steel and leather, Eileen Gray, 1920s.

● **BELOW** Chest, Eileen Gray, 1920s.
Strong geometry, luxurious materials and good workmanship characterize these Modernist designs by Gray.

urious domains for the playing out of office dramas against impossibly immaculate shiny floors; likewise dance routines would proceed over similarly sparkling floors. The filmgoing public became used to seeing furniture which was unobtainable in any shop but which had about it elements of the Moderne. Consequently, the style began to gain much more popularity in the United States than it had before the 1930s. More and more consumers began to be surrounded by versions of the Moderne in public places and associated such surroundings with popular movie stars. Moderne ultimately began to be connected with the glamorous world of Hollywood and films, a fact which did nothing to harm its popular appeal, particularly in the United States.

The predilection for designers using the Moderne style in public places continued in the United Kingdom with the refurbishment of London's Strand Palace Hotel in a hybrid of Deco and Moderne

influences, brought together by the designer Oliver Bernard in 1930. This was a classic example of the employment of a design technique in which the geometrical ornament of sleek stainless-steel and chrome surfaces was pushed to the fore (the hotel's staircase and doors are now exhibited in the Victoria and Albert Museum in London). The move away from the mechanistic aspects of furniture design is perhaps no better illustrated than in the output of British firms like Practical Equipment Limited (PEL) and Cox and Co.

The previously mentioned move from the operating theatre to the cocktail bar was, in Great Britain at least, made by these two companies, PEL and Cox. Once more there was an immense intermingling of design skills employed in transforming what was originally conceived as austere, practical and functional furniture into the type of artefacts which could grace the lounge of the Metropole Hotel in Brighton, or be sold in London stores like Harrods

●**ABOVE** Staircase at the Strand Palace Hotel, London, Oliver Bernard, 1930.
A classic piece of Moderne design incorporating marble, chrome and illuminated panels of plate glass.

and Heals. Designers who worked with the PEL company included Edward McKnight Kauffer, his textile-designing friend (later his wife) Marion Dorn, Arnold Clark, Duncan Miller and Betty Joel. PEL took part in the Ideal Home Exhibition in London in 1932, bringing the sturdiness and attractive design qualities of their tubular-steel furniture to the notice of the ordinary British public. Oliver Bernard, of Strand Palace Hotel fame, was engaged to design their London showrooms, another step in the firm's pursuit of a stylish and modern image. The fact that Bernard was at this time also designing furniture to be produced by the rival Cox and Co was of really no consequence, but it once more illustrates the way in which ideas in design were circulated and given popular currency between the wars.

In 1931 the London-based architects Wells Coates and Serge Chermayeff visited the Dessau Bauhaus, where work on tubular steel construction and the principles of cantilevering were included in the 'Vorkers', or foundation year, which all students had to go through. Although the pair were well acquainted with the principles of cantilevering through their architectural work, their visit to the Bauhaus may well have been an influence on future work. In such subsequent commissions as the furnishings of the new Broadcasting House for the

● **ABOVE** Chairs with aluminium frames, Marcel Breuer, 1932.
Once more bordering on the Moderne, Breuer's chairs employ what was then an expensive material, aluminium, to achieve a modern yet functional design.

● **BELOW** Baby grand piano and stool, 1930.
A pure Moderne design in white lacquer for the cocktail lounge.

BBC in London (in which Raymond McGrath also had a hand) and Wells Coates's studios and blocks of flats, the functional elements of Bauhaus thinking were in evidence.

Wells Coates's pedigree prior to his work at the BBC included a seminal example of modern design in a new material called phenolic plastic or Bakelite. The AD65 radio for Ekco (produced from 1934) was a radical departure from the design of radio cabinets in England: completely circular, it boasted little ornamentation, save for the patinated effect of the plastic surface. Coates employed a functional aesthetic in the simple shape of the case, which was doubtless much easier to mould than a more complex design. At the time it would have been seen as a design exhibiting quasi-functionalist traits, with its form and material placing it directly into the modernistic arena. Indeed, this radio has become an acknowledged classic of modern design.

Modernistic design found currency in other media too, notably in ceramics. The works produced in the 1920s by Clarice Cliff (1899–1972) for the firm of A J Wilkinson in Staffordshire have also enjoyed a resurgence in interest. Cliff was trained at the Burslem School of Art (in the pottery-making Staffordshire district of England), where her tutor,

● **BELOW** Newport Pottery/ Wilkinson Pottery, 1930s. Jugs and figures displaying popular images of the home, the craze for dancing and some motifs which are distinctly redolent of De Stijl – however inappropriate for the decoration of a jug.

● **OPPOSITE** Skyscraper furniture, set of drawers, Paul T Frankl, 1920s.
Architectonic furniture for the larger home or office was designed by Frankl, a New York designer, for the age of the skyscraper. Such pieces incorporated the stepped motif which had become so characteristic of that built form.

● **BELOW** Novelty aeroplane cigarette lighter, 1930s.
The spirit of the age is captured in the most mundane of objects.

Gordon Forsyth, believed his student was using motifs from modern art but not fully understanding what they meant. Whether or not there was an element of truth in this, it is undeniable that Cliff's designs tapped into the 'spirit of the age'; indeed, they were advertised, marketed and sold as modern(e). Therfore, when Cliff applied her designs to the more geometrically severe biscuit ware at Wilkinson's, her sense of colour, coupled with her occasional use of designs by established painters such as Laura Knight and Graham Sutherland, placed her work firmly within the lexicon of modernistic design. Cliff's pottery was nothing if not Art Moderne, and would not look out of place in any room furnished in this manner.

Likewise, the Shelley Potteries become one of the foremost proponents of 'jazz modern' pottery for the home. The 'Vogue' range from 1931 was advertised as being 'of the modern age' and the 'Casino' range by Royal Doulton was heralded in advertisements for its 'simple modern lines'. Decorations on these ranges of domestic pottery were often hand-rendered, although sometimes transfers or decals were used. All were characterized by a strong reliance on simple geometrical shapes, lightning flashes and perhaps an exotic glint of silver applied to the rim of a cup or the edge of a saucer.

Standards of design on board the great ocean liners also drew heavily on the influence of the Moderne, notably the work carried out on the flagship of the French merchant fleet, the *Normandie*. Several design teams worked on the interior fittings of this ship. Its swimming pool, measuring 75ft × 18ft (23m × 5.5m), was designed by Patout and Pacon and featured mosiacs, concealed lighting and a dropped sofit in a ziggurat formation. In the first-class dining salon René Lalique designed the lighting in a fashion which was pure Moderne. The opulence of the first-class winter garden also drew on the Moderne vocabulary, using Algerian onyx

and wrought copper. In Britain, too, ocean liners sported Moderne motifs. The ubiquitous Edward McKnight Kauffer acted as a consultant and designed some of the detailing for the flagship of the Orient line, the *Orion*, in 1935, although the commission for the interior went to the architect Brian O'Rorke. The designs for the interior of this ship were so innovative that no company in Britain could be found that was already producing fittings of a suitably Moderne design. Consequently, all the designs had to be made for the liner from original drawings. Such was the social and business cachet inherent in having an intensely Moderne interior in one's new ship that the high costs and great deal of labour entailed did not deter either the designers or the shipping line. Unfortunately, most of this work was shortly lost when the ship was converted for war use in 1939.

The influence – indeed the era of the Moderne in the United States – was also widely felt, disseminated as it was through films, graphics and other mediums. The Moderne found its way into the homes of ordinary American people in much the same way as it did in Britain, although probably more powerful promoters of the style in the United States were the many exhibitions and even world fairs highlighting it. In terms of design the Moderne was executed with flair and opulence, generally coupled with a respect for the tenets of Modernism. For a time the modernistic represented the cutting edge of a search for a truly American style of design, combining the best from both sides of the Atlantic with an aesthetic from the realm of the machine. For example, Hans Knoll had been producing tubular-steel furniture in Germany in 1934 before he moved to the United States and set up the Knoll Associates Company. Therefore his knowledge of furniture production techniques in tubular steel – doubtless coloured by the German lead in tubular-steel furniture design – was brought to a public eager to consume a new and fashionable style.

Figures like Paul T Frankl (1887–1958) and Donald Deskey (b. 1894) loomed large in the world of American Modernist design. Frankl in particular quoted heavily from the classical ideals of Le Corbusier in justifying his designs, and he also believed that the skyscraper represented the apotheosis of modern engineering-inspired design. Consequently, the 'skyscraper' type of furniture was conceived with one foot in the Moderne camp and the other in the Modernist/Machine age camp, drawing as it did from the stylistic thrust of both the work of Le Corbusier and the machine-inspired look of the drawings in Hugh Ferriss' visionary book, *The Metropolis of Tomorrow* (1929).

Donald Deskey was responsible for many of the interiors at Rockefeller Center's Radio City Music Hall, which demonstrated an ability to wed

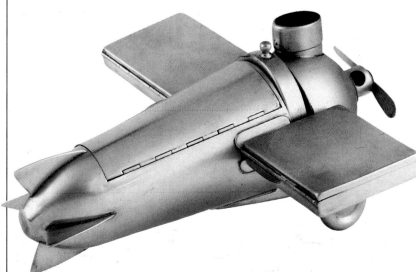

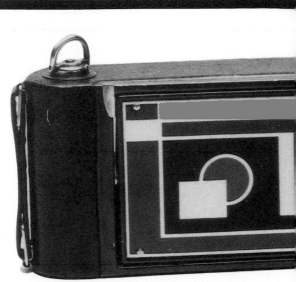

●**ABOVE** Bathroom for Tilly Losch, London, Paul Nash, 1932.
Extensive use of plain and textured glass in pink, purple and black marks this room as a well-realized piece of Moderne interior design.

Art Moderne with a part Art Deco, part machine-inspired aesthetic skill. He brought this to many of his designs, from furniture and lighting fixtures to wallpaper and domestic interiors.

The American Union of Decorative Artists and Craftsmen was formed in 1927 to protect the interests of its members against manufacturers who were used to borrowing from traditional styles for their cheap mass-manufactured goods. The fact that the plastic industry was soon to borrow heavily from the styles conceived by this collection of designers, artists and craftsmen in the production of everyday, moderne-inspired goods shows their lack of success. Where they were successful was in mounting exhibitions of modern American designs, as well as the publication of a journal, the *Annual of American Design*, to which designers such as Bel Geddes and Lloyd Wright contributed.

To a large extent the American fascination with the Moderne is tied in with the search for a truly American design aesthetic. Designers like Raymond Loewy, Harold Van Doren and Walter Dorwin Teague were strongly identified with 'industrial design' and the growth of the corporate image, but they nevertheless contributed to the general 'scrap-book of styles' upon which designers could draw. This occurred in much the same way as in Europe, where designers found themselves in search of a new modern style and hence used other designers who worked in similar idioms as sources for inspiration and justification. Thus the influence of the famous industrial designers was seen to mingle with the works of others, such as Deskey, Frankl, Lurelle Guild, Gilbert Rohde, Gustav Jensen and Joseph Urban. This was then coupled with an allegiance to and knowledge of the principles of design being hammered out in Europe by the likes of Mendelsohn, Chermayeff, Le Corbusier and Mies van der Rohe. The move made to the United States by many of these designers in the 1930s should have made that country the source of all modern designs, but the war intervened and both designers and materials were diverted to the solution of more pressing problems.

● **ABOVE** 'No 1A Gift Kodak' camera, with lacquered wood and chrome box, Walter Dorwin Teague, 1930.
Geometric designs brought the Moderne to many unlikely objects: this camera, along with its box, was transformed by Teague into a highly fashionable accessory.

● **LEFT** Radio City Music Hall, Executive Suite, Donald Deskey, 1930s.
Chrome and leather are used once more in SL 'Roxy' Rothafel's suite. Its style is at once 'American Deco' and Moderne.

Poster for 'La Revue Nègre', Paul Colin, 1925.

CHAPTER SEVEN

ART AND DESIGN: THE POWER AND APPEAL OF THE MODERN IMAGE

● **OPPOSITE** Poster for Bauhaus exhibition 'Art and Technology', Joost Schmidt, 1923.
This image shows the Constructivist influence at the Bauhaus in the early 1920s.

● **BELOW** *For the Voice*, El Lissitzky.
A strong Constructivist image by the Russian artist who taught at the Bauhaus and collaborated with Mondrian on the De Stijl programme.

Within the lexicon of 1920s and 1930s style, some of the most powerfully conveyed sets of images are held within the interlinked worlds of art and graphic design. Posters, illustrations and works of art have become interwoven with the style of these two decades, to the extent that one image is able to evoke a whole range of associations concerning the 20 years in question. It would be almost impossible to pin this phenomenon down to one set of reasons. Nevertheless, it is partially because of the extraordinary way in which, during this rich, highly creative period, various disciplines cross-fertilized each other and grew together. Architects would design typefaces, painters would design houses, graphic artists would create costumes, poster designers would be influenced by architects, and so on. Therefore, while divisions between disciplines were maintained, with artists essentially remaining artists and architects remaining architects, there was a distinct shift in the way in which practi-

tioners within the various fields saw themselves and applied their talents. The prevalent atmosphere, that artists and designers were breaking new ground for a new age, meant that opportunities for experiments in different fields came into being more readily than had previously been known.

Form and meaning within design in general shared motifs derived from a common interest in the redefinition of artistic and design parameters. It was as if a new language had been invented by an avant-garde which keyed into the modern obsessions with the machine and rationality and cut across the conventional boundaries between areas of design, art and theory. This was coupled with a feel for the indeterminable, yet recurrent idea of the 'spirit of the age'.

There were certain events which facilitated the growth of this creative mélange. The setting up of the Bauhaus was one such event. The school was founded in 1919 in Weimar, Germany, under the new regime of the socialist president, Friedrich Ebert, and under the direction of Walter Gropius (1883–1969). It was not so much the thrust of the early Bauhaus teaching, with its attempt to wed art and craft, that makes it so important in this context. More importantly, the school provided a focus for the artistic, creative and intellectual life of post-World War I Germany, which lasted for 14 brief years. At times the school acted as a clearing house for many of the foremost artists and designers in Europe. Indeed, several artists, painters, designers and architects considered prime movers in the world of design between the wars found their way to, and through, the Bauhaus. Paul Klee, Wassily Kandinksy, László Moholy-Nagy, Marcel Breuer and Mies van der Rohe are but a few of them.

Definite links were forged between the Bauhaus in Germany and the De Stijl movement in Holland, led by Theo van Doesburg and Piet Mondrian, and the Vhutkemas (art schools) in Russia, whose teachers included Kasimir Malevich, Vladimir Tatlin and El Lissitzky. This further added to the ferment of design theory and practice in Europe at this time. By the mid-1930s the Vhutkemas, the Bauhaus and the De Stijl movement had all met their demise. The rises of Stalin and Hitler put paid to the avant-garde tendencies of the institutions and movements in central and eastern Europe. These eventualities forced designers and artists to travel and many set their sights on the New World making their way to England as a matter of course and leaving their marks, by way of influence and design and later by practice, in the United States.

This cross-disciplinary influence, which is so characteristic of the interwar years in Europe, can be seen in many instances. In 1920 Paris the Purist movement, led by Le Corbusier and Amadée Ozenfant, determined to produce art which employed

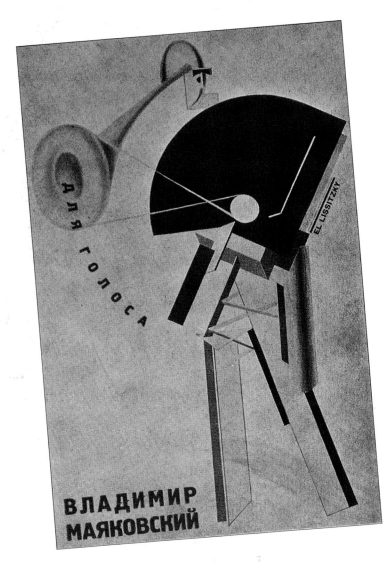

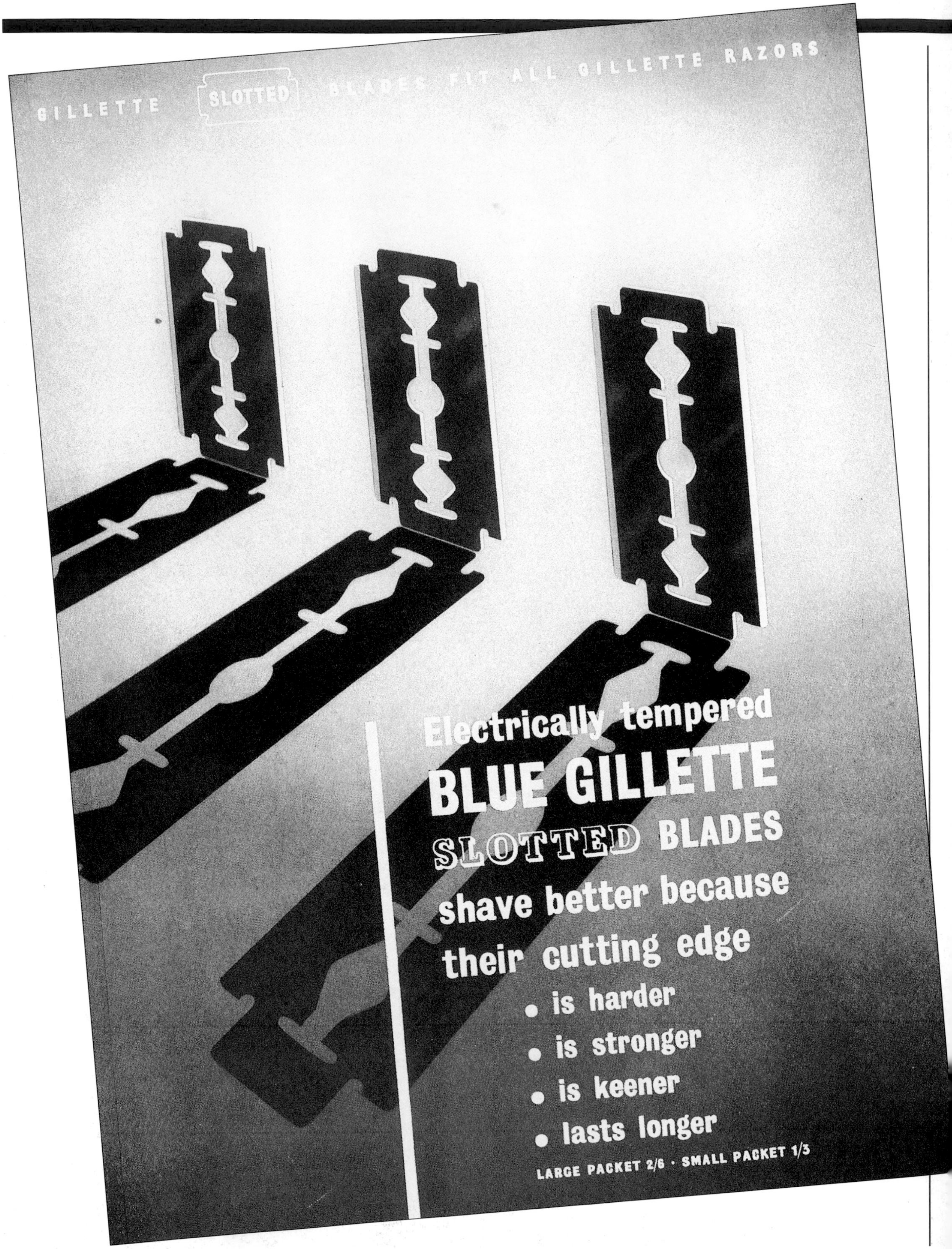

GILLETTE SLOTTED BLADES FIT ALL GILLETTE RAZORS

Electrically tempered
BLUE GILLETTE
SLOTTED BLADES
shave better because
their cutting edge

- is harder
- is stronger
- is keener
- lasts longer

LARGE PACKET 2/6 · SMALL PACKET 1/3

● **OPPOSITE** Blue Gillette advertisement, 1937.
Strong sans-serif imagery had found its way into advertising by the 1930s, with a great deal of information about a product being put across in a very simple way.

● **RIGHT** *Josephine Baker*, lacquer on wood, Jean Dunand, *c*1926.
An image upon which many 1920s artists drew was that of the fantastically popular cabaret star of Paris, Josephine Baker.

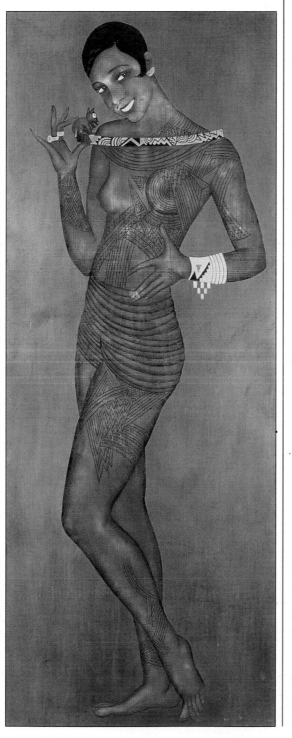

the painting as a 'machine for the transmission of sentiment'. The magazine *L'Esprit Nouveau* was published at this time (from 1920–25) and formed the basis of Le Corbusier's seminal 1923 book, *Vers une Architecture* which contained the similar idea that the house 'is a machine for living'. Fernand Leger, too, professed to be influenced by the machine age and the subjects within his paintings took on the appearance of machined, cylindrical surfaces, far removed from artistic devices which had come before in his work.

In Holland, the founders of the De Stijl movement also produced an eponymous journal to give vent to their own feelings about art, architecture and the world in general. The paintings of Piet Mondrian can be seen as the gradual rationalization of perception and representation into the horizontal, the vertical, primary colours, and black, white and greys. Formally speaking, these ideas broadly tie in with the Modern Movement aesthetic and can be found expressed to their fullest in Rietveld's 1924 Schröder House in Utrecht.

Not an architect but a designer, Gerrit Rietveld (1888–1964) built the house as an exercise in three-dimensional planar composition, in much the same way that he had rendered his famous 'Red and Blue Chair' in 1917, with colour picking out the structural detail. El Lissitzky, the Russian Constructivist artist who had been travelling in Europe during the 1920s, published an article on Rietveld upon his return to Russia in 1925, so aiding the spread and knowledge of avant-garde ideas in art, architecture and design among the students and intelligensia of yet another country.

In Russia itself, the Constructivist movement had its own particular artistic language, adopted as the official revolutionary art. The famous 1920 poster 'Beat the Whites with a Red Wedge', was used (unsuccessfully) as a propagandist tool. Plastered on to trains, it travelled the Russian countryside, largely confusing the peasants. However, for those Europeans attuned to the thoughts behind Constructivism, it represented a reduction and rejection of traditional artistic representation and wedded its purpose to social change and a strong belief in 'the machine'. Consequently, the power of industry – once it was in the hands of the workers – for bringing about change in the social order was the ultimate utopian message. After 1921, when Constructivism was abandoned as the official revolutionary art form and the New Economic Policy was brought into action in the USSR, the artists behind the movement found their ideas had no outlet. However, people like László Moholy-Nagy (1895–1944), who had links with the Constructivists and who were later to become influential in imparting artistic theory and practice to their pupils at the Bauhaus, made sure that the principles of Constructivism were not allowed to die. Rather, they saw them subsumed into the general vocabulary of artistic usage.

Traces of the influence of the Constructivist idea are apparent in many images readily associated with European design during the 1920s. The fact that Constructivism, De Stijl and later Bauhaus ideas were expressed in a strongly geometric formal language only serves to heighten the sense that during the 1920s at least, the abandonment of unnecessary ornament in avant-garde, but obviously not *all* modern design, came to be seen as a powerful art practice and therefore existed to be drawn from as part of a formal language. This was so much the case that in mid-1930s England Russian-born Berthold Lubetkin (b.1901), along with other members of his architectural practice, Tecton, designed a block of flats in Highgate, London, called Highpoint One. They were, Lubetkin conceded, built 'in homage to Braque'. The flats appear as a well-realized piece of white-painted modern architecture, and it is perhaps certain repeated motifs in the balconies and other details which represent the inspiration the architect found in the work of Braque. Nevertheless, it is enough that Lubetkin chose to acknowledge the influence of another artist. It demonstrates the use and currency of modern formal languages as points of intersection between different disciplines.

A particularly strong distillation of current visual languages between the wars can be found in the work of the poster designers in Europe and England and, to a lesser extent, in the United States. Adolphe Jean-Marie Mouron (1901–68), better known to the world by his pseudonym Cassandre, is now perhaps the best known of the European poster designers. Certainly his work is regarded as among the most evocative of the period – and it was arguably the most successful in its own time. Between 1923 and 1936, Cassandre used the poster as no one before him had. In his hands it represented an interface between the visual languages of the avant-garde and the ordinary public. The adept use of the pictogram, bold typeface and skilful lithography meant that a combination of the elements of Constructivism, Cubism and Modernist design in typeface came together as a commercial tool and, some would say, a work of art.

Cassandre's self-confessed love of architecture was borne out by the fact that he lived in a concrete house designed by Auguste Perret, an architect acknowledged as one of the originators of pre-stressed concrete construction, the method favoured by Modern Movement architects. This sensibility was then coupled with a hatred of what he called 'deforming details' and no doubt coloured the way he approached his subject matter. It is no accident, therefore, that some of his most enduring images were produced to advertise railways and shipping lines. After all, these posters were to represent the very machines which inspired the architects, which in turn inspired the artist. Thus, Cassandre's posters for *Nord Express* (1927) and for the ocean liner *Normandie* (1935) represent the opposite ends of Cassandre at his most concise. This was the time when his work most reflected and utilized the current modern machine aesthetic-inspired visual language. As representations of distilled 1920s and 1930s style, they are hard to better.

Cassandre was by no means the only poster artist operating in Paris. Indeed, when this period in

● **ABOVE** Poster for the *Compagnie Générale Transatlantique*, Cassandre, 1935.
This poster, together with that for the French train service (opposite page), represents a style which Cassandre made his own. Strong, direct pictogrammatic images conveying mood as well as information became his trademark.

sign system. This in turn was seen to underline the existence of a common ground shared by forward-thinking designers in all disciplines.

The formal language adopted by, for want of a better term, the avant-garde in Europe at this time cannot be viewed in isolation from the rest of the world of art. Indeed, the boundaries of what was possible and – what is more – what was acceptable in terms of visual representation were opening up every day. The artistic language developed by Braque and Picasso had been realized relatively early in terms of the period in question. Cubism, as a recognizable artistic style, existed by about 1915, but between the years 1920 and 1928 Picasso was still producing large Cubist still lifes, like *Three Musicians* (1921) and *Three Dancers* (1925), which were, by then, very much a part of acknowledged

● **RIGHT** Poster for the
Compagnie des Wagons-Lits,
Cassandre, 1920s.

Paris is discussed, it is often in terms of the three 'C's: Cassandre, Colin and Carlu. Paul Colin (1892–1985) is perhaps most famous for his poster for 'La Revue Nègre' of 1925, the show which introduced Josephine Baker to Paris. These posters were in a style slightly reminiscent of that of Marc Chagall, the artist who had been the Art Commisar of Vitebsk in Russia in 1919 and was succeeded by Kasimir Malevich when the Vhutkemas were set up in 1920. Colin's style took a similar route, moving away from figurative representation to a style which was inspired by Constructivism, consisting of overlapping planar surfaces. This style is particularly in evidence in his work for the Wiener and Doucet Piano Company. Before this, Colin designed a series of posters to advertise Josephine Baker's recordings. Baker, the American-born exotic dancer, was another pivotal figure in 1920s Paris, having a garish black-and-white-striped house designed for her by the proto-Modernist Viennese architect, Adolph Loos, who also designed a house for Tristan Tzara, the poet and Dadaist.

The third 'C', Jean Carlu (1900–83), can also be seen as a representative of the verve, vitality and adaptability of creative people in Paris at this time, untrammelled by the idea that one discipline was enough. Carlu trained as an architect but, after losing his right arm in an accident, gave up architecture and moved into poster design. His output was of a similar standard to Cassandre's and Colin's but gravitated towards less glamorous goods, 'Mon Savon' soap of 1927 and consequent advertisements for toothpaste being among his most successful executions. Another artist operating in Paris at the same time, designing both posters and packaging, was Pierre Fix Masseau, whose Cassandresque style in the French Railways *Exactitude* poster in 1932 served to underline the effectiveness and popularity of this style.

Until the advent of commercial radio after the war, the poster campaign was by far the most effective way of reaching a mass audience and informing them of the product on offer. Of course, the realization that, in a world dominated by the poster, new posters had to be simple and powerful just to get their message across must have had an impact on the way that the poster was conceived. That there was a 'scrapbook' of visual ideas available to the poster artists to draw upon, in the guise of avant-garde art and architecture, was only to their benefit.

In England the poster was also the primary means by which products could be sold and information disseminated. Among the primary exponents of the art of the poster in Britain was Edward McKnight Kauffer (1890–1954), an expatriate American who settled in London in 1914. Kauffer thought of himself as a painter until 1921, the year his work as a poster designer took off and he was

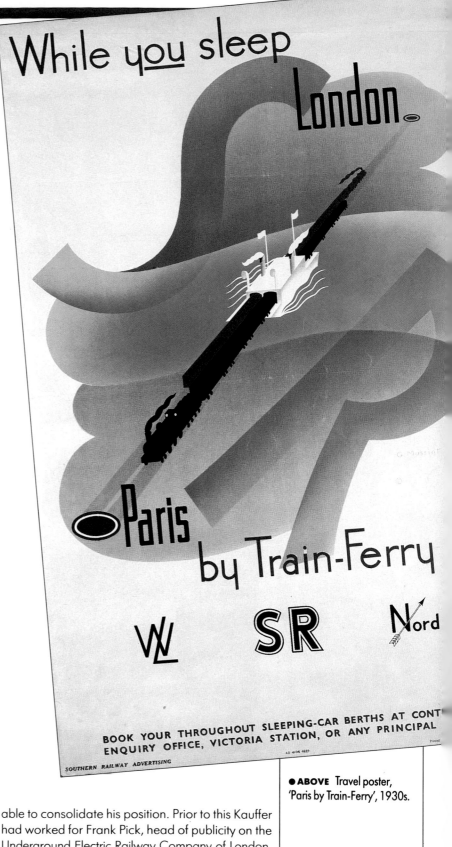

able to consolidate his position. Prior to this Kauffer had worked for Frank Pick, head of publicity on the Underground Electric Railway Company of London, producing posters of Watford, Reigate and other rural places accessible by London Transport. These posters depended on a relatively simple, but stylized representation of a landscape to suggest the idea of day-tripping to a nearby ideal spot. Kauffer's poster design, *Flight* (1916) is markedly different

● **ABOVE** Travel poster, 'Paris by Train-Ferry', 1930s.

● **RIGHT** '6 and 12', E McKnight Kauffer, 1930s. This image by Kauffer is an intelligently designed inducement to use what was an expanding and modern Underground system. The modernity of the graphics reflects the modernity of the means of transport.

from these transportation images: a highly stylized representation of a flock of birds, it was inspired by a Japanese print as well as marked by the influence of the Vorticist movement, which flared briefly in World War I London. It appeared in *Colour* magazine, which devoted one page per month to a poster design. The design was later taken up to advertise a national newspaper in 1919.

By the mid-1920s Kauffer had consolidated his position in Great Britain as a leading poster designer; indeed, in 1925 there was a retrospective exhibition of his work featuring 56 of his designs. After this point Kauffer's work expanded to meet the influence coming from the continent, taking on board the motifs which are today so readily associated with this era. Edward McKnight Kauffer also pioneered techniques of photomontage, collaborating on several occasions with the celebrated photographer, Man Ray, who was well known to the smart artistic set in Paris. Kauffer further illustrated the tendency for designers to work in more than one medium by his designs for rugs (his wife, Marion Dorn, was a celebrated rug designer) and his collaboration with architet Wells Coates on the wall mural at Embassy Court, Coates' seaside block of flats in Brighton (1935). He even designed book jackets, among them one for HG Wells' *The Shape of Things to Come* (1935), later made into a film. This work, along with posters, murals, rugs and illustrations helped to place him firmly in the category of 'modern designer'. Although he and Dorn returned to the United States in 1940, Edward McKnight Kauffer found his most notable success in the United Kingdom, where he always, however, acknowledged his American roots. Poster designers who originated in Britain included Fred Taylor and Frank Newbould, whose travel posters were characterized by the use of flat colours and stylized representations of well-known spots in Britain.

So far, images and cross-disciplinary influences have been discussed in terms of the poster in Europe. In some ways the poster and design in general across the Atlantic was to be deeply affected by the migration of artistic and design talent from Europe, as the Nazis became more and more powerful and Europe became an increasingly difficult place in which to exist. The list of names that finally found their way to the United States reads like a design hall of fame for Europe.

The Russian émigré Erté (born Romain de Tirtoff in 1892) gained lasting fame as a designer – first in Paris and later in the United States. Between 1924 and 1937, he was exclusively contracted to design covers and illustrations for *Harper's Bazaar*. Working in a manner closely allied to Parisian Art Deco, Erté – both the man and his designs did much to convey a fashionable European sophistication among other American magazines, a highly desirable ability

when Europe was in vogue as *the* fashionable place. Erté also worked in other disciplines, continuing the penchant for the multimedia designer. Consequently, the success of his stage sets, fabric designs and graphics meant that he attained unparalleled status on two continents as a designer with his finger on the pulse of European-inspired Art Moderne.

Once settled in the United States, other European designers found their voices in the pages of fashion magazines. Notable among them was the Russian-born poster designer, Alexey Brodovitch (1898–1971) who had been working in Paris but who was the art director at *Harper's Bazaar* from 1934. He employed the likes of Salvador Dali, Man Ray and Henri

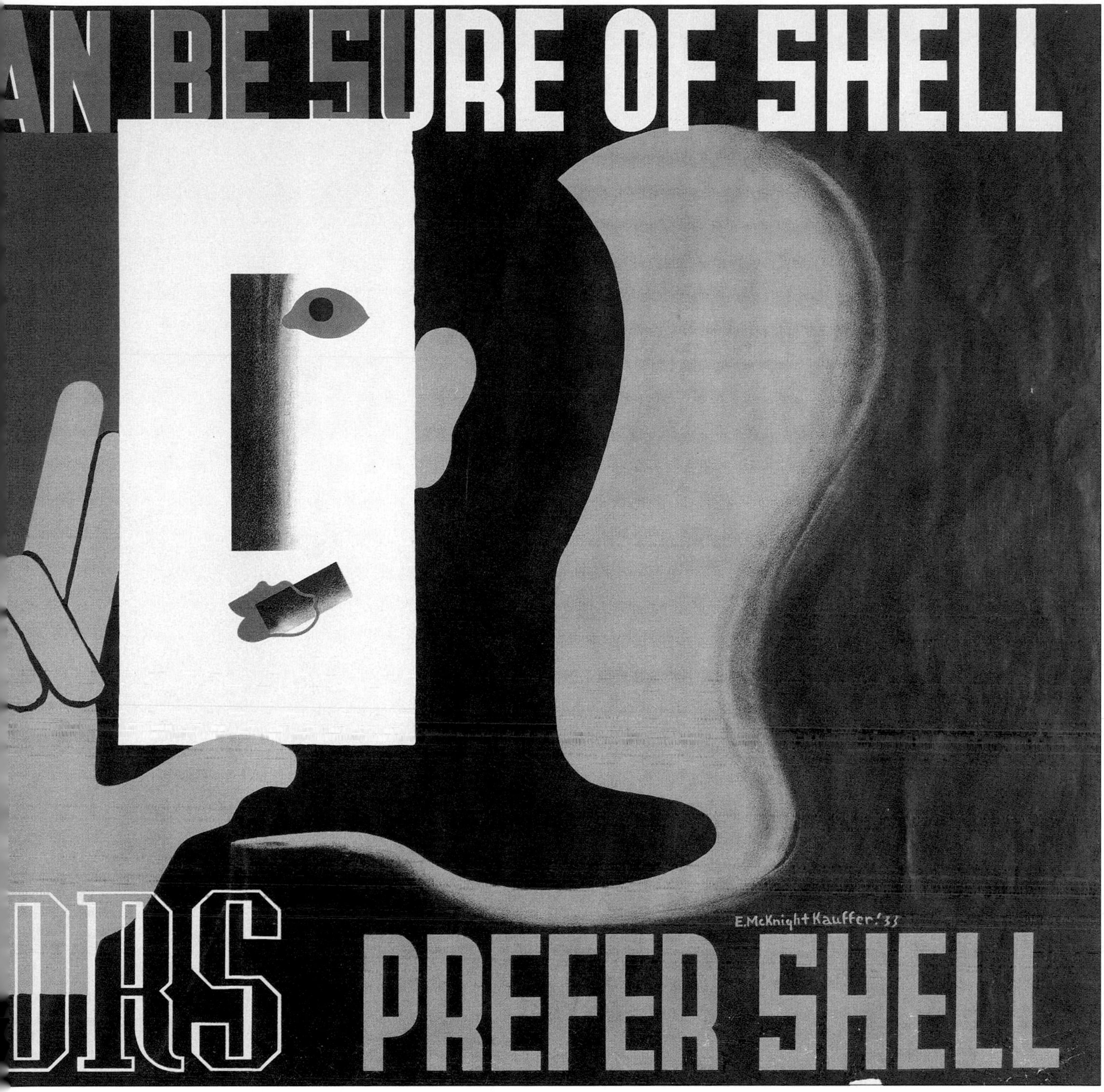

Cartier-Bresson to provide photographs and, with consummate skill, fundamentally altered the rules governing the way magazines were to look.

As far as home-grown American talent was concerned, the field was dominated by Lester Beall, a self-taught graphic artist whose clever use of photomontage and Modernist typefaces helped to promote, among other things, the Works Progress Administration (WPA), which was part of Roosevelt's New Deal from 1935. By this time Beall was surrounded by European talent: Cassandre, Mondrian, Carlu, the artists Max Ernst and Marcel Duchamp, Bauhaus teachers Gropius, Herbert Bayer, Breuer and Moholy-Nagy, and photographers Man Ray and Cartier-Bresson. Clearly at this time in the United States the thrust for innovative graphic design was coming from Europe. Even famous American graphic icons, such as Raymond Loewy's bold design for the 'Lucky Strike' cigarette pack in 1940, owe a great deal to the influence of Bauhaus-inspired sans-serif graphics. Even the official posters for the 1939 New York World's Fair, depicting the quintessentially American image of the Trylon and Perisphere, came from the pen and airbrush of an expatriate Austrian, Joseph Binder. He, too, drew heavily from the 'scrapbook' of Modernist and avant-garde images forming the basis of 1920s and 1930s style in the graphic arts.

'The Polo Game', fashion- plate, 1923.

CHAPTER EIGHT

FASHION:
FROM COCO CHANEL TO
READY-TO-WEAR

The story of fashion in the 1920s and 1930s has often been represented as exclusively that of the major couture houses located in Paris. But the names of Schiaparelli, Paquin, Worth, Channel and Balenciaga represent but one facet of what amounted to a growing obsession among the women and, to a lesser extent, the men of the world.

Far from being the domain of the upper classes, stylish new fashions were seen to percolate through every social rank in terms of clothing, hair and various accessories. Furthermore, the fashion of the upper – as well as the middle and lower – classes was to a certain and unprecedented extent affected by the modish dress and appearance of the newly created, larger-than-life film stars. For perhaps the first time, orginality and novelty in fashion came from more than one source and what was fashionable and accepted as such could just as well originate from Hollywood – say, from the smart geometric haircut sported by Louise Brooks, or the sexy pyjama suits worn by Marlene Dietrich – as from the French fashion journals. What is difficult to determine is where the impetus for actual change in fashion came from, and whether the stars of stage

and screen were a reflection of or a model for popular taste. The answer is that they were probably a combination of both, but immeasurably significant was the way in which style was disseminated to a huge audience.

In addition to the films, the growth of the women's magazine industry, particularly in the United States, provided an outlet for information and a stimulation for demand. *Vogue*, *The Queen* and *Harper's Bazaar* all contributed to a fashion consciousness which, until the late 1920s at least, the ordinary woman had been aware of, but as something beyond her own sphere of experience. Now, for many more women than before, there existed the opportunity to be 'fashionable' in a way which was truly a part of the swiftly changing modes and morals of the day. In short, the art of being fashionable was made easier by the fact that what was fashionable in the 1920s was so radically different from what had gone before.

The quest for contemporaneity could start with something as simple as a haircut. The bob, with its associations with modernity and rejection of the encumbrance of flowing locks, was a truly 'today'

● **BELOW LEFT** 'The Seaside', *Art-Goût-Beauté*, 1921. A fashion-plate for couture clothing featuring designs by (left to right) Molyneux, Beer, Doucet, Jenny, Doucet, Beer, Molyneux, Beer, Molyneux.

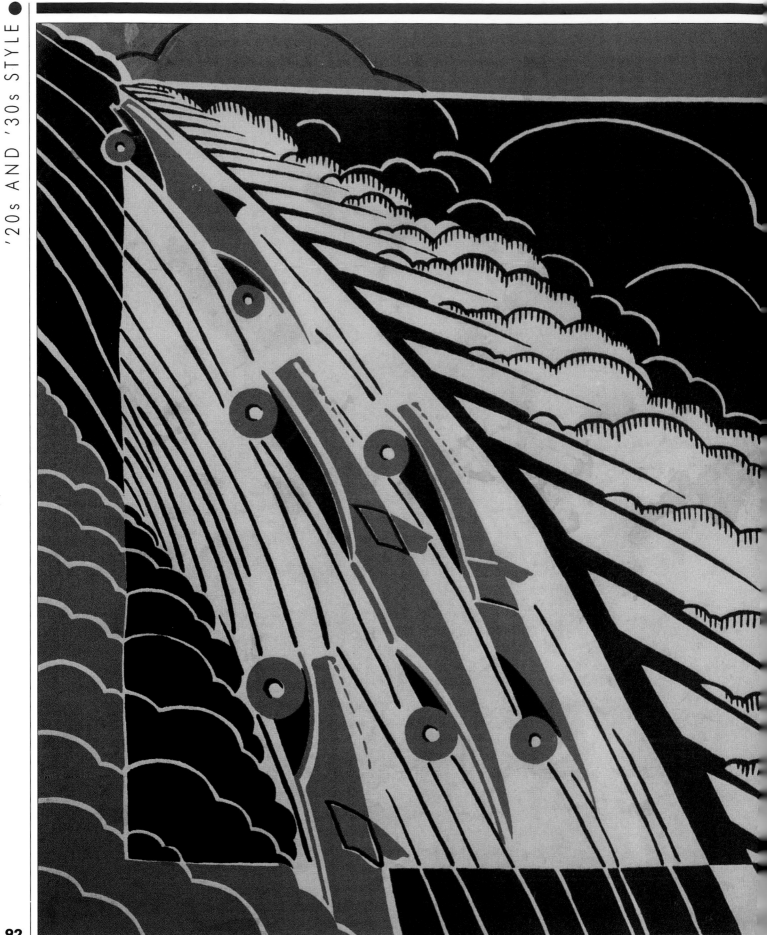

●**LEFT** Headscarf,
1920s/30s.
Automobiles, speed and
modernity all collide in this
most modern of
headscarves.

●**RIGHT** Advertisement for
Helen Jardine, 1920s.
The woman illustrated in this
advertisement sports a
turban (first made popular
by the couturier Paul Poiret),
Cupid's-bow lips and heavy
eyeshadow. As such, she
exemplifies the union of
couture and Hollywood in
the creation of a fashionable
look.

HELEN JARDINE

FASHIONS = AND COMMERCIAL ART

hairstyle for the modern woman. After 1924 it was swiftly superseded by a more dramatic version of modern haircutting techniques: the so-called 'shing-ling' of hair resulted in a shorter effect at the back, whiile maintaining a 'traditionally' feminine length on the top and fringe. For a time there was another alternative in the shape of the 'bingle' – a cross between the bob and the shingle which assisted in the transition betwen the styles for those who were not quite so daring as to take the plunge into 'shingledom'. The ultimate and most severely modern hairstlye arrived towards the end of the 1920s and was dubbed the 'Eton crop', due to its similarity to the haircut worn by boys at the famous English school. The hairstyle consisted of a short back and sides, a small quiff at the front and often a side part. The progression had moved from short to shorter to shortest. After the Eton crop there was nowhere left for the fashionable female head to go and so for a while in the early 1930s, it became

fashionable to grow one's hair.

Hairstyles were always closely allied to other elements of prevailing fashion, and the reason for the shortness of the modern hairstyles in the 1920s may lie in the shift of the ever-changing focus on areas of the body as erogenous zones. Once again the movies can be seen to play a role in this change in public taste.

The vamp was born in silent American films of the early 1920s, best realized by the likes of Pola Negri and Theda Bara. Because of the nature of acting for soundless film, attention was focused on the eyes as tools of expression and dramatic effect. Kohl-rimmed orbs would glare in close-up from under exotic turbans or bandeaux pulled down over the brow and further accentuating the glowering, submissive, terrified or lustful stare of the ruby-red-lipped leading lady. It is no great leap to make between the look of the vamp under her turban, bandeau or close-fitting hat and the popularity of

93

the face-framing cloche hat which endured for most of the 1920s. Since this hat was worn by the majority of women, it is not surprising that long hair – too voluminous to be stuffed under the heat-hugging cloche – was all but forced out of the picture.

Perhaps the most dramatic change in women's clothing was in the length of hemlines, which had been modestly low at the beginning of the 1920s but which shortened as the decade progressed. By 1925 the hemline had risen from the ankle to the knee, and once more the shifting erogenous zone was in evidence as the long-hidden female leg came boldly into view. What is more, it made its appearance clad in stockings, which were very often in flesh-coloured silk or the newer, excitingly modern (and not to mention cheaper) rayon. This material was also used for underwear and evening dresses, and between 1920 and 1925 its production rose from 8-million lbs to over 53-million lbs in the United States alone! This increase gives some idea of the success and widespread usage of the novel material which was limited almost exclusively to the arena of clothing.

The shortening hemline and the subsequent display of the female leg can be allied, albeit tenuously, to the increasing emancipation of females, relating to both their consciousness and behaviour. What were then the newly fashionable dresses were related to the acceptance of jazz music in certain circles and the ability to move to the music was of paramount importance. The reign of types of dress which were restrictive in this way came swiftly to an end, for the young and fashionable realized that it was impossible to do the charleston in a hobble skirt or the black bottom in a whalebone corset.

Although the silhouette of the fashionable female was not subject to all of the rigours it had been in the previous century, the shape of the body was still conditioned by the restrictive foundation garment called 'the flattener'. This was a device worn over the bust to literally flatten the profile of the woman, thus giving her a boyish physique commensurate with the fashionable boyish hairstyles. This in turn allowed for the 'tube dress' to take precedence. This dress had a look paying no heed to the natural 'ins and outs' of the female body: the bust was non-existent; the waist dropped to just on, or just below, the hips; the skirt was short, focusing all the attention onto the legs. A fashionably short hairdo or cloche framed the face, long earrings and necklaces glittered and danced, bangles were worn en masse, snaking their way up newly exposed arms. And to complete the look, a decorative powder compact was wielded, perhaps carried in a smart beaded bag. There was also the mass acceptance of the fashionable 'jumper'. First sold around 1922, the jumper was to form an integral part of the young woman's wardrobe. Generally it was worn pulled

down around the hips with a blouse underneath and a short pleated skirt. In terms of everyday fashion, this look was to endure to the end of the decade, and it is important, too, because it was a look transcending the boundaries of class.

The difference between mass fashion and couture, though, were realized through the types and qualities of the materials used. The luxury of evening dresses and the social life that demanded them were of course the realm of high fashion and the rich, the glittering arena which the names of Coco, Chanel, Elsa Schiaparelli, Balenciaga and their haute-couture contemporaries come into their own. For although some of their designs would

● **ABOVE** Poster for the Royal Mail Line, 1924. Showing the change undergone in men's fashion and giving an impression of popular male dress in the mid-1920s.

Chosen·by·Travellers·
of·Discernment·in·
1924

MAIL LINE
YORK & SOUTH AMERICA
PING EXPERIENCE
M PACKET COMPANY

skirts which had reached their zenith of shortness at the peak of the Jazz Age, the so-called Roaring Twenties. Perhaps it was the effects of the great slump, but the 1930s witnessed a dissolution of the single style for fashionable women and an embracing of many different styles both in Europe and North America. Short hair and the cloche hat lost their supreme positions and were replaced by longer, wavy locks and the small hat perched rakishly on the side of the head. This was accompanied by the lengthening of skirts until the hems were, on average, 10 ins (25cm) above the ground. The one concession to fashion which every woman was to make, regardless of the style or detailing of the rest of her dress, was in the waist. The return of the boned corset was eventually interrupted by the demands on both bodies and materials occasioned by the outbreak of World War II. The small waist was, more often than not, complemented by an exaggeration in the width of the shoulders, a look in part prompted by Joan Crawford.

In terms of haute-couture and evening wear, the area of emphasis shifted once again and the back came into its own. Indeed, even some daywear was slit at the back to show bare skin. This trend grew alongside the general passion for sport and sportswomen, which was especially strong in the 1930s. In swimming and tennis, for instance, the clothes worn by both professionals and amateurs became much more practical and because of this, more revealing. It was during the 1930s that female tennis players first appeared at Wimbledon minus stockings, but the furore which greeted this spectacle quickly subsided with the acknowledgement of its practicality. The growth of golf as a game for both men and women also meant that fashionable ladies were seen attired in practical and not just decorative clothing on the links. The growth of sunbathing and the belief in the beneficial effects of a suntan – as well as its social cachet – also meant that for those on the beach, flesh had to be revealed rather than concealed.

In terms of men's clothing, cut had resolved itself by the mid-1920s and the greatest changes to occur were in the choice of materials. The suit continued to be a staple part of the average man's wardrobe, but there was a distinct and growing move towards the casual, which continued through the 1920s and into the 1930s. Notwithstanding the elegance of the upper-class male in top hat and tails, personified by Fred Astaire and countless real-life models, the everyday man was seen in the lounge suit, which changed in small details. By the mid-1920s, the waistcoat had grown out of favour, prompting the move to the double-breasted coat. By the end of the decade the waistcoat was back, worn double-breasted under a single-breasted coat.

By far the most outrageous change in the cut of

eventually affect the contents of the ordinary working girl's wardrobe, their most immediate sphere of influence extended into the beau monde, of which they were a distinct part. Indeed, Schiaparelli was renowned for her concept of introducing styles inspired by honest working clothes into high society, once more shifting the impetus for change in clothing fashion. Schiaparelli became big business, and it has been estimated that by the end of the 1920s the House of Schiaparelli, with its 26 workrooms employing over 2,000 people, was turning over more than a hundred million francs a year.

The beginning of the 1930s saw a turnaround by the leaders of fashion, who sought to lengthen the

men's clothing between the wars was in the width of the trousers. The Oxford Bag, so called because of its origination and adoption by the undergraduates of Oxford University, gained rapid popularity but diminished by the end of the 1920s; however, the width of the trouser leg was to remain relatively wide until the end of the 1930s. There were other menswear novelties, among them plus fours (short trousers generated for shooting and adopted for golfing and then for town wear), the motoring cap, the boater and the blazer. All these were rather peripheral developments in the world of men's fashion clothing, however, and were set against the same changing backdrop of social and economic upheaval which characterized these fashion-fixated years.

Of course, the buying of clothes was made easier with the introduction of ready-to-wear clothing and catalogue shopping, the latter initiated by mail-order houses like Great Universal Stores or Sears, Roebuck. This system allowed payment by installment, thereby making all types of clothing and fashion accessories accessible to those on a limited budget.

It has often been pointed out that during the 1920s hemlines rose in inverse proportion to the stock market, so that by the Great Crash they were at their highest while stocks and shares had reached an all-time low. While this is not necessarily a phenomenon that begs serious analysis, it does offer an example of the world against which fashion was playing out its ephemeral role. It was a time of harsh realities, deprivation and hunger for many people in the Western world, and yet in spite of this – or maybe because of it – fashion flourished and gained importance on a hitherto unequalled scale. With the hunger marches, the General Strike, the Great Crash and the world recession which ensued, fashion and being fashionable offered a cushion against that world – that is, for those lucky enough to be relatively unaffected by these crises.

● **LEFT** Marlene Dietrich. The actress is 'wearing a beige kasha and sheer brown wool suit. Note, the skirt length is new . . . Miss Dietrich's hat is brown felt adorned with a single goose quill'.

● **OPPOSITE** Deco-style printed headscarf incorporating silver thread in the weave, 1930s.

'Transatlantique' poster for *Compagnie Générale Transatlantique*, 1930s.

TRAVEL:
FROM OCEAN LINERS
TO FLYING BOATS

● **OPPOSITE** Poster advertising the 'quick steamers' *Bremen, Columbus* and *Europa*, post-1928. These vessels were designed to win the coveted Blue Riband for Germany.

● **BELOW** Italian liner, *Rex*. Italy's only Blue Riband holder, *Rex* took the record from the German liner *Bremen* in August 1933.

In terms of 1920s and 1930s style, the world of transportation offers many innovative examples of artefacts which were stylistically very well realized. Whether or not this is a consquence of form following function is not a matter for discussion here; suffice it to say that, in capturing the stylistic essence of the two decades in question, it would be difficult to find better models than those thrown up by the designers of means of travel.

In the 1920s and '30s, the world came to be under the influence of increasingly nationalistic governments. Policies implemented by the governments in Italy, Russia, Germany and the United States were intent on stressing the difference between countries rather than promoting a spirit of international cooperation. Yet, paradoxically, this was the age when relatively rapid and reliable intercontinental travel was to become more of an everyday reality than ever before. Travel, and with it the means of travel employed, came to represent a very particular model of modernity. It was a model which, for the few who could afford to travel in style, also embraced ideas of luxury and convenience.

For the masses, the reality of travel was third class, by train, boat or ancient car. For these people, long-haul destinations were generally for the purposes of immigration, to escape destitution or persecution at the hands of governments and economic systems which paid little or no heed to the third-class citizen. For the great majority of people, then, their picture of travel in style was conditioned by the knowledge that there was a class of people who would travel for pleasure or business but who would do so in comparative comfort. These were the people who were not the 'huddled masses' welcomed by the inscription on the brow of New York's Statue of Liberty; they were an élite, small in number and definitely privileged. Nevertheless, their presence and their use of ocean liners, airships, luxury trains and fast cars as modes of transport did much to contribute to the popular perception that the world was, in effect, shrinking.

The increase in navigability of the world's seaways and, later, airways meant that the public perception of travel was conditioned by the glamour of highly visible, highly publicized, nationally backed ventures. On the sea, the 1920s and 1930s spawned some of the greatest and most nationalistically inspired modes of transport in the shape of the ocean liner. Regular scheduled crossings of the North Atlantic had been made since the 19th century but it was not until the 20th that the crossing could be made with anything approaching modern 'speed'. The speed in which the Atlantic could be crossed was a focus for both publicity and national pride. The fact that the British Liner, the *Mauretania*, had held the 'Blue Riband' for most of the early 1920s was to spark a great nationalistic battle, with the Atlantic Ocean as the battlefield and the liners as weapons. The publicity value of holding the Blue Riband for the Atlantic crossing was inestimable, in spite of the fact that by the end of the 1930s differences in crossing times were being measured in hours rather than days.

Such was the lure of this prize that in 1926 Germany decided to attempt to regain the Blue Riband by making a conspicuous attempt to build the fastest ships the world had yet seen. Two ships, the *Bremen* and the *Europa*, were laid down that year and completed two years later. They were

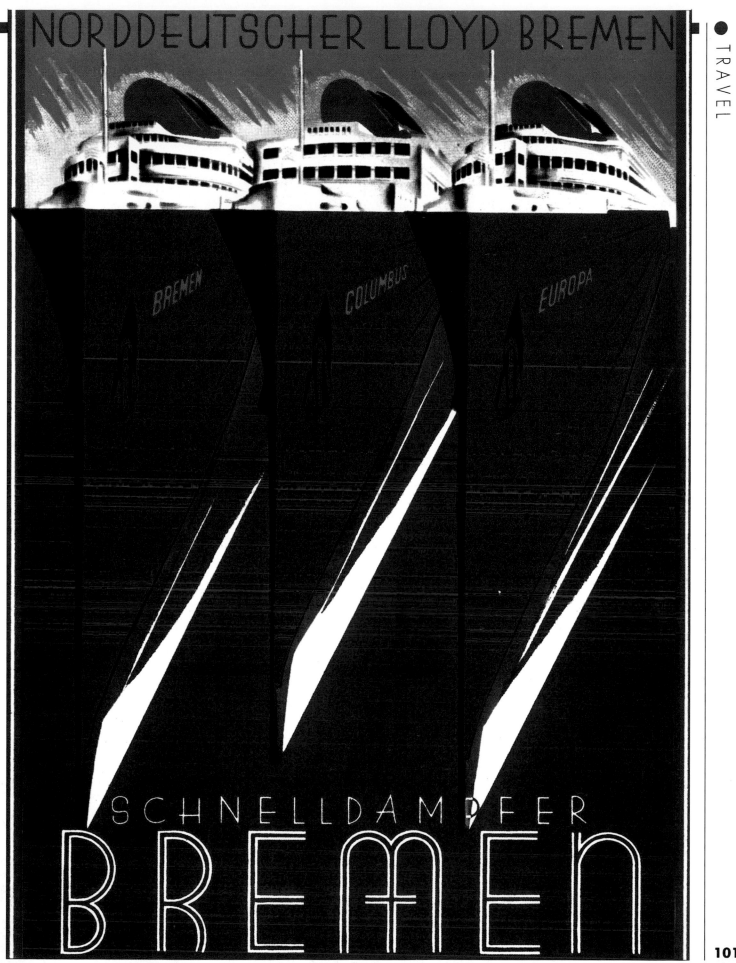

● **ABOVE** The huge glass mural designed for the interior of the Grand Salon on the French liner *Normandie*, 1932.

● **RIGHT** The Grand Staircase leading up to the statue *La Normandie*, on board the French liner of the same name.

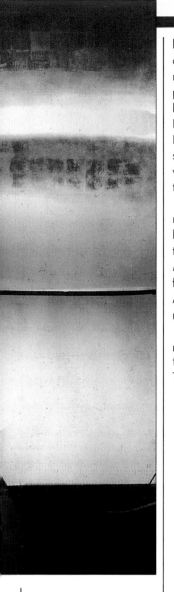

launched just one day apart on the 15th and 16th of August 1928. The attempt at the Atlantic crossing record was also an attempt at rebuilding national pride within Germany, and it was successful, at least on the first count, when the *Bremen* took the Blue Riband on her maiden voyage from Bremen to New York. For the next 10 years the two German ships were untouchable, except for one slight hiccup when the Italian liner *Rex*, flying Fascist colours, took the westbound honours in 1933.

The German domination of the North Atlantic run was ended by the competition generated between Great Britain and France, with their ships the *Queen Mary* and the *Normandie*. The *Normandie* was launched in 1932, but the Depression following the Wall Street Crash caused the *Queen Mary* to be delayed for over two years. She was not launched until 1934.

The design of the *Normandie* was radically modern and included turbo-electric power and the then-innovatory squat-raked funnels, three in all. The first-class dining salon was 305ft (93m) long

and seated over 700 fare-paying passengers. Altogether she could accommodate over 2,000 travellers spread over first, tourist and third classes.

Ownership of the Blue Riband alternated between the *Normandie* and the *Queen Mary*, with crossing times hovering around the four-day mark. A measure of the importance of these ships as messengers of national superiority and general objects of interest can be gained by the size of the crowds that witnessed their arrivals in New York, particularly on their maiden voyages. These ships were well designed for the task they had to perform, a statement proven by the fact that in 1938 the *Queen Mary* was to set a record for the crossing which would stand until 1952, when the *United States* would overtake her.

The *Queen Elizabeth*, the not-quite-sister ship of the *Queen Mary*, had orginally been designed to be identical to her predecessor. However, such was the march of progress in steam-turbine technology that by the time the *Queen Elizabeth* was launched in 1938, the turbines had been improved to the

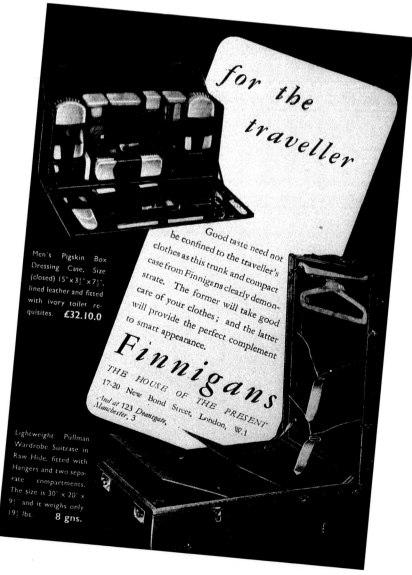

Men's Pigskin Box Dressing Case. Size (closed) 15″ x 3½″ x 7½″, lined leather and fitted with ivory toiler re-quisites. **£32.10.0**

Good taste need not be confined to the traveller's clothes as this trunk and compact case from Finnigans clearly demonstrate. The former will take good care of your clothes; and the latter will provide the perfect complement to smart appearance.

Finnigans
THE HOUSE OF THE PRESENT
17-20 New Bond Street, London, W.1
And at 123 Deansgate, Manchester, 3

Lightweight Pullman Wardrobe Suitcase in Raw Hide, fitted with Hangers and two separate compartments. The size is 30″ x 20″ x 9½″ and it weighs only 19½ lbs. **8 gns.**

● **LEFT** Advertisement for Finnigans travelling cases, 1939.
Increased possibilities of travel over wider and wider distances meant that the modern voyager had to be well-equipped.

103

extent that only two funnels were needed. The *Queen Elizabeth* did not see civilian passenger service until after World War II, and so the weekly service operated by the two ships, planned a decade earlier in the heyday of the liners, was not to be realized.

The impact of the ocean liners on the consciousness of an already style-conscious world is well in evidence throughout this period. The white-painted superstructure, hand rails and clean lines of the exteriors can be found echoed in much of the marine and Moderne architecture of the period. The interiors were seen to echo the most sumptuous of the buildings found on land, particularly in areas reserved for the first-class passengers. Floating palaces to some, symbols of a modern age to others, the liner as machine was championed as a source of inspiration by the architect Le Corbusier. They were represented in advertising as the epitome of everything modern and stylish, and to travel first class became the fashionable way to cross the Atlantic. They also carried with them the sometimes more sinister messages of nationalism and superiority, both in class and international terms.

Although by far the most popular, the liners were by far the most comfortable. In 1919 the R34, a British dirigible, or steerable, airship made the first round trip across the Atlantic and back between Edinburgh and New York. It was based on a German design, the L33, which had been captured at the end of World War I. After this quiet, inauspicious, militarily derived trip, no airships were to cross the Atlantic until 1924, when the German ZR3 was sent to the United States as a partial payment under the terms of the reparation agreement for war damages. Under similar terms, Italy had taken

three airships from Germany, but had managed to crash all but one of them by 1922. Italy's intention in accepting the airships in lieu of payments had been to set up a commercial airship service between Rome and Italian-controlled Tripoli in North Africa. It was the potential for the use of airships in linking colonies and empires which became one of the prime motivating forces behind their research, development and construction.

The British Army Major Scott, who had commanded the successful transatlantic jaunt by the R34 in 1919, had the idea for an airline linking London with Cairo, Port Said, Bombay, Rangoon and Singapore. For this task, he wanted the British government to sponsor the building of an airship bigger than anything hitherto envisaged. Due to bureaucracy and muddled management of the project, what Scott ended up with were two airships: the R100 and the R101. Both ships were twice the size of anything that had flown before. Work was begun in 1926, and by the time the aircraft were finished in 1929 the R101 was only 50 ft (15m) shorter than the ocean liner *Mauretania*. At 709 ft (216m), this huge airship was more than twice as wide in the beam as that liner.

In 1930 the R100 crossed the Atlantic in 78 hours. The R101 had rather less luck, being despatched to India for political expediency. On her way, just 220 miles (352km) into the journey over Beauvais in France, the R101 crashed, killing 46. In 1931 British involvement with airships ceased with the dismantling of the R100. However, this withdrawal did not signal the end of the worldwide interest in airships and their potential.

Two German ships, the *Graf Zeppelin* and the *Hindenburg*, continued to operate as fare-collecting,

● **ABOVE** The *Graf Zeppelin* at Hanworth Airfield, England, August 1931.

● **OPPOSITE** Poster for Deauville, France, 1930. The advertisement was designed to attract tourists to Deauville by any means possible – by plane, by boat, by car, by train.

● **ABOVE** Empire Flying Boat *Circe* taxies in Southampton Water.
The Flying Boats cut the journey time to South Africa (the Cape) by a third.

mail-carrying cruise ships. Flights to West Africa and South America were frequent. In the 1930s the President of the United States, Franklin Roosevelt, allowed a special revocable permit for the *Hindenburg* to land at Lakenhurst, New Jersey, and so the swastika, the symbol of Nazi Germany, was seen against a backdrop of New York skyscrapers. At this time the Chrysler Corporation ran an advertisement showing the *Graf Zeppelin* over the Chrysler Building in New York, with the tag line, 'ultra modern transportation and architecture'. Despite the fashionability of the ultra-modern, the dramatically reported crash of the *Hindenburg* at Lakenhurst on 6 May, 1937 effectively put an end to public confidence in the possibilities offered by airship travel. Although smaller, infinitely less glamorous blimps were used in World War II the days which had seen the *Graf Zeppelin* making a majestic low pass down the Unter den Linden in Berlin, or the R100 over London on its way to far-flung Empire colonies, had gone forever.

For a short while, airships had represented much more than the opportunity to shrink the world for the lucky few who were able to fly on them. Given that, in the 1930s, the price for travelling 'the triangle',

from Germany to South America to the United States, was in excess of $6,500. Their worth to ordinary people was like that of the ocean liners; they were a focus of pride in a nation's achievements as well as a dramatic and memorable sight in the skies. The airship represented at once a contemporary modernity and a potential for the future conditioned by man's mastery over distance and the elements. The demise of the airship due to public concern about its safety was aided by the increase and efficiency of long-distance powered flight.

One of the truly enduring symbols of the 1920s and 1930s style is the flying boat, or early aeroplane. Both in Great Britain and the United States the flying boat came to represent a faster alternative to travel by ship and was indeed the precursor of long-haul flights which seem so much a part of everyday life today. On board a ship, a journey from England to Australia would take more than a month. When in 1935 the first scheduled air service between London and Australia began it, too, was not cheap, with a one-way ticket costing £195. The bonus was in the fact that instead of spending five weeks at sea, the journey time was reduced to 12½ days. The mid-

1930s were the boom period of the flying boats as technology improved to allow long-distance flights with a modicum of comfort for the passengers. The first American flight by a flying boat linking the mainland to Hawaii, was made by a Boeing 'Clipper' class aircraft in April 1935. This initial flight represented a longer-term plan to link the American mainland with the Philippines – and therefore extend both the American sphere of influence and the international perception of what the United States as a nation could do.

In Britain, the first of the Short Brothers' 'Empire' Class Flying Boats flew for Imperial Airways in October 1936. Such was the potential for speedy travel to faraway destinations that Imperial Airways ordered 28 of these new aircraft. Significantly, the company was seen to be gambling on the success of a regular, scheduled air route to the Far East. The effect of setting up such an ambitious, long-distance route was once more twofold: it provided a swift mail link to Britain's empire interests in the Far East, notably India, and in so doing re-affirmed the nation's

place on the world stage. It was also, for a short time, a profitable commercial venture for the airline. A flying boat silhouetted against the pyramids on the Nile did much for the corporate image of an airline based in Southampton Docks.

When Imperial Airways first set up these 'colonial' routes, the journey was made in sections, often involving travel over land or sea to the next aircraft. The advent of the new flying boats, like the Short 'C' Class, meant that travel became less broken and the opportunity for a touch of luxury arose. Given that no transfers needed to be made, life on board these aircraft had to be made as bearable as possible for the fare-paying passengers. Consequently, there were stewards on hand to serve the travellers, night sleeping accommodation, and 'downstairs' a smoking lounge, equipped with settees and wicker furniture for the 17 or so passengers who would make the journey. It was unusual for passengers to make the full trip all the way to Australia; some would join the plane and travel for a few 'stages'. Therefore, profits for the airline were

● **RIGHT** Poster for Imperial Airways, 1930s.
Advertising the exotic and far-flung destinations reached by the Flying Boats and more conventional aircraft.

● **RIGHT** Commemorative pin for Charles Lindbergh's historic solo air navigation across the Atlantic Ocean in 1927.
The plane is a representation of Lindbergh's craft, *The Spirit of St Louis.*

NEW YORK TO PARIS
MAY 21, 1927

KING OF THE AIR

more often than not made through carrying mail. Such was the demand for mail carrying that often the smoking lounge would be closed to passengers and filled with mail bags.

Flying boats in the United States told a similar story but, if anything, the standards of comfort aboard the American 'Clippers' surpassed their British equivalent. Passenger quarters aboard the Boeing M130 Clipper had steel double washbasins and comfortable bedding. Passengers ate from china plates and were attended by bow-tied stewards. Once more, wicker chairs were used in the lounges, ostensibly for their lightness, and they did much to contribute to the stylish image of tropical glamour associated with travel by air.

However, the reality of two weeks in a flying boat may well have been less glamorous than we have come to think of it today. These planes were noisy and sluggish and the facilities offered to the passengers, although good for an aeroplane, fell far below those to be found on an ocean liner. Their major advantage lie in their relative speed. By the time of World War II, a plane could cross the Atlantic in 15 hours, as opposed to four days on a ship. Likewise, flights to Hong Kong from Alameda, California, could be completed in a matter of days rather than weeks.

Between the wars, the realm of transport contained many 'firsts'. It was a time of growth and innovation in many areas and ways of travelling were at the forefront. Henry Ford started the first

American freight service in 1925. The first commercial air-mail flights in that country were made by Varney Speed Lines in 1926. Technological developments affecting just what an aircraft could do in terms of capacity, speed and manoeuvrability were occurring all the time all over the world. The first airlines were begun in the United States, and where before distances had prohibited the growth of a good communications network relying on rapid transit of goods, mail and people, the United States was pulled together as never before.

This was also a time of pioneers, particularly in the field of aviation. In 1927, Charles Lindbergh became a genuine all-American hero when he landed his tiny plane, *The Spirit of St Louis*, in Paris, after completing the first non-stop solo crossing of the Atlantic Ocean. Amelia Earhart achieved the same feat in 1932.

If Earhart the aviatrix represented yet another facet of the growing and generally perceived emancipation of women, the phenomenon existed as a further example of how something as initially mundane as transport and transport design impacted upon the consciousness of nations and hence the world. The fact is that because of the innovatory nature of much of transport design, it was able to transcend the mundane and symbolize the quintessence of modernity. Through travel and ways of travelling, some nations were conquering distance, whereas those with more expansionist tendencies were conquering other nations.

General Motors, 'Highways and Horizons' model street intersection (Norman Bel Geddes, consultant), 1939.

CHAPTER TEN

THE NEW YORK WORLD'S FAIR: THE ENDNOTE OF 1920s AND 1930s STYLE

The New York World's Fair, held in 1939 from 30 April through October (and reopened in 1940 for another six-month period), represented the conglomeration and display of American know-how — in the larger-than-life guise of a machine aesthetic-based vision of the future. It was the apex — and some say the death knell — of the previous two decades, obsessions with the machine and art, the progress of mankind, the future and the quintessential modernity of the day. Although it contained exhibits from all over the world, the New York World's Fair was really a celebration of everything American. From ingenious futuristic pavilions to the omnipresent automobile, the fair exhibits carried on a tradition started by the Great Exhibition in London's Crystal Palace in 1851 of promoting, if not political, then cultural imperialism. The host country was seen to harbour all the future aspirations of the world, while other countries were represented as lesser entities, such as quaint villages (in the case of England) or merely by their cuisine (Poland and Holland).

Although a major theme of the Fair was distinctly future-orientated in content, its other main function was to serve as a marker for the 150th anniversary of the birth of democracy in the United States, when George Washington became the first President of the country in 1789. The inference was that the United States was about to democratize the whole world, and that the future was safe in the hands of the US. As it would later come to pass, American involvement in the protection of the democracies of several countries was to prove crucial after 1941, but the fair paid no heed to the idea of war. Instead it presented vistas of almost implausible advancement to an eager populace. It showed a present and a future in which the public wanted to believe, and as such represented an opportunity for the distillation and packaging of the modern American 'world' in a way which had not been attempted before.

The New York World's Fair was an immense organizational coup, a fitting end to 20 years of technological progress and, largely, peace. Although Europe had already witnessed the bloody civil war in Spain and the expansion of Hitler's territories with the Anschluss, the United States was enjoying a period of relative stability and regrowth after the years of the slump. All around there were ready examples of American progress and building,

● **RIGHT** Trylon and Perisphere, New York World's Fair, 1939.
The New York World's Fair site from the air, showing Trylon and Perisphere and giving some idea of the scale of the exhibition.

● **LEFT** The Trylon and Perisphere viewed at night.

● **RIGHT** In contrast to the noble and lofty appearance of the Trylon and Perisphere surrounded by statuary, the symbols were also used in more mundane ways, as shown by these plastic salt and pepper shakers.

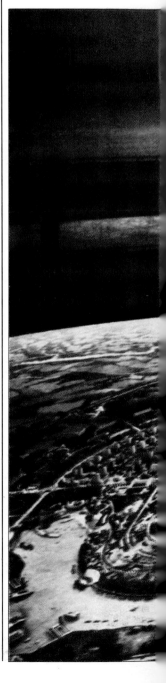

such as the massive dams and turbines photographed for *Life* magazine by Margaret Bourke-White. The mood was optimistic; the country, it seemed, was back on course.

The decision to hold the World's Fair came by way of a fund-raising venture on a non-profit making basis in order that a new park could be built at Flushing Meadows in Queens, New York, for use by the inhabitants of the city. As an undertaking by New York City, the Fair offered the opportunity for the presentation of America to Americans in a fully designed environment. Because the site was started from scratch, every aspect of it was intended to display the hallmarks of modernity. It was all an integrated and orchestrated attempt to package 'the American way' – and perhaps to convince the American public that they should maintain their faith in 'the American dream'.

As this was essentially the packaging of a nation,

it seemed natural that the men who were to do the packaging should be the country's industrial designers. Thus, many of the major attractions at the Fair, and a good deal of the minor ones, were conceived and realized by the offices of Raymond Loewy, Norman Bel Geddes, Henry Dreyfuss and Walter Dorwin Teague. It was almost as if the often visionary work of these designers was being vindicated by their inclusion in such a massive world event. They were in effect designing the country they wanted the world to see, a country located in the present, its eyes firmly set on the future.

The Fair was a mixture of amusement park and trade exposition, with the larger American corporations heavily investing in the presentation. The fact that several of the nation's industrial designers were already contracted to General Motors, Ford, Westinghouse and other major firms meant that, as well as being involved in an official capacity as consult-

● **BELOW** The huge scale model that was 'Democracity', designed by Henry Dreyfuss as a predictive model for life in some imagined future.

ants to the Fair's design, further unity was achieved with the commercial exhibits originating from the same pens and brains.

The Fair itself employed modern ideas from its inception. It was zoned, a concept much in vogue in futuristic and utopian urban design, and it had integrated transport systems which fed the zones. Railways were custom-built for the Fair, run by the City Subway Company and the Pennsylvania Railroad – 'From the World of Today to the World of Tomorrow in Ten Minutes For Ten Cents' ran the slogan of the PRR. Raymond Loewy designed special Greyhound buses to ply the 25 miles of specially built roadway, plus there were electronically powered 'motoguide chairs' for hire, driven by college graduates. The site covered a massive 1,216 acres

and was patrolled by 2,000 World's Fair Police, but, boasted the guide book, 'every area is readily and quickly acessible'.

Two 'theme buildings', the Trylon and the Perisphere, dominated the Fair, and also doubled as its symbol, appearing on the posters which publicized the event. The Trylon was simply a 700-ft (213-m) high marriage between a triangle and a pylon and symbolized 'the Fair's lofty purpose'. The Perisphere was a functional building and housed one of the show's most intriguing exhibits. Two hundred ft (61m) in diameter, the Perisphere was home to 'Democracity', a model conceived by Henry Dreyfuss to go inside Harrison and Fouilhoux's vast (twice the size of Radio City Music Hall) dome.

Visitors to the Perisphere stepped onto what was

● **ABOVE** Futurama in the General Motors 'Highways and Horizons' exhibit. Designed by Norman Bel Geddes, unsurprisingly this vision was of a future city largely dependent on the automobile.

then the longest moving staircase in the world, thence were borne upwards to emerge onto one of two balconies revolving in opposite directions. From this moving vantage point the visitor would watch a six-minute-long show, designed to represent a vision of a 'perfectly integrated, futuristic metropolis' of a million inhabitants. After two minutes of mini-ature bustle and city life, with tiny cars zooming along tiny (but to scale) multilane highways, 'dusk' fell over the 'Democracity'. The domed roof became illuminated with stars. Then, at ten equidistant points around the dome's walls, giant projections of groups of marching workers appeared, obviously returning from their toil in the fields and factories of 'Democ-racity'. All this drama was further heightened by a

thousand-voiced choir, which was accompanied by a full orchestra performing a symphony specially composed by William Grant Still as the theme song for the Fair. The figures, having grown to 'mammoth size', then disappeared behind the drifting clouds, and the show ended with a 'blaze of polaroid light'.

Inextricably allied to the 'lofty purpose of the Fair', the Theme Center – with 'Democracity' at its heart – was an exercise in 'futurological' propa-ganda stemming from a distinctly American view of the way things should be in an ideal world. The *official* Guide Book read: 'Visitors will never forget it, symbolical as it is of the age old quest for know-ledge, increased leisure and happiness . . . The Fair may help to build a better world for tomorrow by

making its millions of visitors aware of the scientific knowledge and the forces and ideas at work in the interdependent society of today and by demonstrating the best tools that are available'. It is difficult to reconncile this lofty and admirable idea with some of the more bizarre exhibits at the Fair, such as 'Nature's Mistakes', which saw various natural 'freaks' of the animal world paraded in a pit of front of a paying audience. A hog without any ham, a bull with elephant feet, a steer with its heart in its neck and a cat with 28 toes and 28 claws all were marched in front of the crowds. The main attraction at 'Nature's Mistakes' was the bull with human skin; skin so thin, proclaimed the posters, that you could see its veins.

Part 'World of Tomorrow' and part 19th-century fun fair, the New York World's Fair was partially born of the American tradition in huge expositions, consolidated with the idea of the state fair from the previous century. This was then blended with ideas which had first come together at the Century of Progress Exhibition in Chicago in 1933.

The New York World's Fair was nothing if not cosmopolitan and Salvador Dali, in his anagrammatical guise of 'Avid a Dollars,' had set up the exhibit 'Salvador Dali's Living Pictures'. It is easy to imagine the surreality of an extravaganza such as the New York World's Fair appealing to Dali. Twenty-five cents gained admission to a room in which the artist himself, described as 'lively' in the guide, took

the audience on a tour of his 'secrets': *Soft Watches, Piano Women, Anthropomorphic Seaweed* and the momentous *Exploding Giraffe* all held the audience spellbound, while a couch shaped like Mae West's lips and the *Living Liquid Ladies* revealed another side to Dali's extraordinary character.

This meeting of art, industry, the futuristic and entertainment is underlined by a cursory look through other attractions on offer. The self-explanatory 'Temple of the Jitterbug' combines in its title the pre-occupation with grandeur and an altogether more populist approach. The 'Theater of Time and Space' was involved with the world of Buck Rogers and Superman, as it took visitors on a trip through the universe at a simulated 480,000,000,000,000,000,000 miles per hour. On the other hand, and on a more serious note, the Bendix Lama Temple exhibit was intended to raise money for the Committee for Relief of Chinese War Orphans.

The character of the exhibits at much of the Fair was dominated by the interests of big business and the designers who worked for them. Carrying on the theme of the future and the future city, the General Motors exhibit, 'Highways and Horizons', designed by Normal Bel Geddes, contained yet another huge model of a city, this one called 'Futurama'. Containing over a half million 'individually designed houses' and 50,000 scale-model automobiles, 10,000 of which were moving along the highways, 'Futurama' was about the transport of

● **RIGHT** Spectators enjoying the pageant that was 'Futurama'.

● **OPPOSITE** National Cash Register Building, New York World's Fair, Walter Dorwin Teague, 1939.

● **RIGHT** Du Pont Building, New York World's Fair, Walter Dorwin Teague, 1939. Teague was retained as a consultant and designer to the Fair as a whole.

the future, designed at the hands of GM. It was the largest scale-model of a city ever constructed. Visitors toured the exhibit on moving chairs designed to give the impression of aircraft flight and the illusion that hundreds of miles had been covered. In these 'magic chairs' the audience flew over lakes and mountains, towns and cities. In another section of the building, in a spiral ramped room constructed from copper, glass and rosewood, the latest-model Chevrolets, Pontiacs, Buicks, Oldsmobiles and Cadillacs were displayed.

Architecturally, the New York World's Fair contained some striking examples of modern streamlined buildings, the looks of which were obviously conditioned by their functions as exhibition buildings. Windows on many structures were omitted, since this would interrupt the exhibition space on the interior walls. Therefore, the construction of buildings such as the Perisphere or GM's 'Highways and Horizons' (by Albert Kahn) derived much of their unbroken modern line from functional design consideration. Other buildings were simpler and more straightforward but with striking added elements, such as Teague's National Cash Register pavilion, topped by a massive mock-up of the machine they produced. Likewise, the Radio Corporation of America (RCA) building was conceived in a similar vein, but was more subtly realized. Based on the shape of a giant radio tube, it was set into lovely landscaped gardens. It contained an exhibit of television equipment which was being made available to the New York public to coincide with the World's Fair, further underlining the modern aspect

of the Fair's intention.

By far the largest exhibit was that of the railroads, with a working 4,000 horsepower diesel as the centrepiece of an exhibit whose architects were Eggers and Higgins, with the ubiquitous Raymond Loewy as consultant. Inside a thousand-seat hall *Railroads at Work*, a huge model railway and diorama demonstrated – however improbably – the entire operation of a modern railway system. Covering 17 acres in all, the Railroads Buildings also displayed full-scale engines, which obviously required a great deal of that space. Despite being the largest exhibit, however, it was unlikely that it matched the inventiveness, spectacle and vision of 'Democracity' or 'Futurama'.

A major *raison d'être* of the 1939 New York World's Fair was to draw in paying visitors by way of entertainment and information in order to raise funds for a public-works project (alas, the Fair Corporation lost huge sums of money). The only remnants of the Fair today are in the shape of concreted roads, since the architecture, designed as large-scale ephemera, was never intended to last (although some structures of the 1964–65 New York World's Fair, held on the same site, still stand). However, the New York World's Fair did represent a distillation of an American ethos which grew up and flourished in the 1920s and 1930s. The Fair dealt with the future, the machine, art and design, and showed a concern for the future of humanity, though unfortunately this was more often voiced in grandiose terms which ignored the internal problems faced by the country and the world at large.

119

● **ABOVE** Apartment house at General Motors exhibit, 'Highways and Horizons'. 'Modernism' was clearly the style favoured as the architecture of the future.

Still, the New York World's Fair capped the end of the 1920s and 1930s in a memorable fashion. It was a natural successor to the trend for large expositions which had carried on from the 19th century and into the modern age. The Fair was in essence a combination of and improvement on every international exposition of the past. It had elements of the Century of Progress Exposition in Chicago in 1933, the fair which saw R Buckminster Fuller come to the fore as a designer of streamlined vehicles, in his Dymaxion range of cars. Similarities between the New York and Chicago Fairs were underlined by the involvement of many of the same architects and designers. Principally, the Chicago Exposition took a retrograde look at how far the nation had come since 1833, and although the look of the Chicago Fair was broadly in line with Modernist tendencies in art and architecture, it remained primarily an exercise in back-slapping and morale-boosting, soothing a country which was in the depths of the post-slum Depression.

Somehow, though, its 'house of tomorrow' must have rung a little hollow to the viewers who could never imagine being in a position to live in it. Nonetheless, the Chicago exhibition represented a shift in American consciousness: it was an acknowledgement that big business was the source of recovery, it capitalized upon the idea of industrial design, and it heralded the acceptance of Modernism in art and design in the United States, albeit in a form which had swiftly displayed distinctly American characteristics.

In this way the New York World's Fair shared common ground with what has come to be seen as a seminal exhibition – the *Exposition des Arts Décoratifs et Industriels Modernes* in Paris in 1925. The brief of the Paris exhibition was that its displays should be modern in both their conception and execution. As has been shown, the New York World's Fair followed similar guidelines, with modernity the uppermost ingredient in a consolidation of American design and consumption.

● **BELOW** Ford Mercury sign at the entrance to the Ford exhibit.
Note the large glass wall of the 'Modernist' Ford building.

● **RIGHT** Westinghouse display of electrical appliances in the home of tomorrow, New York World's Fair.
Pride of place in the 'Hall of Power' went to the 'Precipitron', a device for attracting household dust electrostatically and at the push of a button.

Lastly, the New York World's Fair shared a common purpose with the London Exhibition held at Wembley in 1924. The Empire Exhibition was an exercise in imperialistic grandeur, a totting up of the dominions and colonies of the United Kingdom in an atmosphere of postwar consolidation. In its dismissive treatment of undeveloped, unindustrialized countries, the New York Fair was simply reflecting a commonly held misconception about the way in which societies from what are now called Third World countries were seen to operate.

The message of the New York World's Fair was one of superiority gained through technological progress. The world, although not owned politically by the United States, was rapidly becoming even more reliant on her resources for financial support. The Flushing Meadows exposition represented an encapsulation of everything that had put the country in this powerful position, from the world of design and the power of the corporate image, to the innate, and propagandized, belief that the United States of America represented, simply, the apotheosis of civilization. The New York World's Fair was more than just a fair; it was a fitting endnote to two decades which had seen immense shifts in the way the world came to work. The world hovered on the brink of war and yet, in the summer of 1939, inside the gates of this temporary shrine to modernity, the future shone brighter than ever before.

121

YEAR	DESIGN	POLITICS
20	● Mendelsohn's visionary Einstein Tower built in Potsdam ● Tatlin's Monument to Third International unveiled	● Founding of the League of Nations
21	● Kandinsky joins the Bauhaus	● Chinese Communist Party founded
22		● Mussolini's March on Rome (October)
23		● Hyper-inflation rampant in Germany ● The French occupy the Ruhr Valley
24	● Surrealist Manifesto published ● Gerrit Rietveld builds the Schröder House in Utrecht	● Lenin dies ● Introduction of Dawes Plan for European recovery
25	● *Exposition des Arts Décoratifs et Industriels Modernes* in Paris ● Bauhaus opens new premises in Dessau	
26		● Germany admitted to the League of Nations
27	● *Weissenhof Siedlung* built in Stuttgart ● Le Corbusier publishes *Vers une Architecture*	
28	● Le Corbusier's Villa Savoye completed	
29	● Hugh Ferries publishes *The Metropolis of Tomorrow* ● Chanin Building opens in New York	● Introduction by Stalin of the first Five-Year Plan ● Trotsky expelled from the USSR
30	● Chrysler Building opens in New York	● Depression sets in in Europe and the United States
31	● New York's Museum of Modern Art holds International Style exhibition	
32	● Publication of *The International Style* by Hitchcock and Johnson ● Norman Bel Geddes publishes *Horizons*	● Franklin Delano Roosevelt elected President of the United States
33	● 'A Century of Progress' exhibition held in Chicago	● Hitler comes to power
34	● Chrysler 'Airflow' hits the road	
35	● Raymond Loewy's 'Coldspot' refrigerator first sold ● Douglas DC3 introduced	
36		● Spanish Civil War breaks out
37	● Golden Gate Bridge built ● *Exposition Internationale des Arts et Techniques* held in Paris	
38		
39	● New York World's Fair held	● Outbreak of World War II

EVENTS	ENTERTAINMENT	YEAR
		20
	● Rudolph Valentino stars in *The Sheik*	21
● Discovery of Tutankhamen's tomb by Howard Carter	● British Broadcasting Corporation begins programmes from Alexandra Palace, London	22
		23
	● George Gershwin's 'Rhapsody in Blue' performed for the first time	24
● John Logie Baird demonstrates his TV system in London	● Charlie Chaplin in *The Gold Rush* ● Eisenstein's epic *Battleship Potemkin* ● Josephine Baker's Paris début	25
● General strike in United Kingdom ● Valentino dies	● Fritz Lang's *Metropolis* released	26
● Lindbergh flies solo across the Atlantic	● Al Jolson stars in *The Jazz Singer*, the first talkie	27
● Discovery of penicillin	● Walt Disney's *Plane Crazy*, featuring Mickey Mouse	28
● New York Stock Exchange fails in the Great Crash		29
● Five million unemployed in Germany	● New Victoria Theatre opens in London	30
	● Charlie Chaplin's *City Lights* released	31
	● Lang's *The Testament of Dr Mabuse* ● Greta Garbo stars in *Mata Hari*	32
	● *Gold Diggers of 1933*, with choreography by Busby Berkeley	33
	● Claudette Colbert stars in Cecil B De Mille's *Cleopatra*	34
● Malcolm Campbell captures World Land Speed Record in 'Bluebird'	● Dick Powell features in *Gold Diggers of 1935*, Fred Astaire in *Top Hat*	35
	● BBC begins high definition TV broadcasts ● Alex Korda's production of HG Wells' *Things to Come*; Chaplin's *Modern Times*	36
● Exhibition of 'Degenerate Art' organized by the Nazi Party in Munich	● Walt Disney's *Snow White*	37
● Sir Nigel Gresley's 'Mallard' locomotive tops 126 mph	● Orson Welles' radio production of HG Wells' *The War of the Worlds* ● The birth of Superman	38
	● Première of Berthold Brecht's *Mother Courage* ● *Gone with the Wind, The Wizard of Oz* released	39

INDEX

Page numbers in *italics* refer to relevant captions

FURTHER READING

Adam, P, *Eileen Grey*, Thames and Hudson, London, 1987.

Banham, R, *Theory and Design in the First Machine Age*, London, 1960.

Barnicoat, M, *Posters; a Concise History*, Thames and Hudson, London, 1988.

Battersby, M, *The Decorative Twenties*, Studio Vista, London, 1971.

Bel Geddes, N, *Horizons*, Dover Books, New York, 1977.

Bernstein, M A, *The Great Depression*, Cambridge Press, New York, 1987.

Brinnin, J M & Gaulin, K, *Grand Luxe, The Transatlantic Style*, Bloomsbury, London, 1988.

Burness, T, *Cars of The Early Thirties*, Chilton, London, 1970.

Camard, F, *Ruhlmann, Master of Art Deco*, Thames and Hudson, London, 1984.

Foucart, B; Offrey, C; Rubichon, F; Villers, C, *Normandie*, Thames and Hudson, London, 1986.

Gallo, M, *The Poster in History*, Hamlyn, London, 1974.

Goldberger, P, *The Skyscraper*, Allen Lane, London, 1982.

Hannah, F, *Ceramics*, Bell and Hyman, London, 1976.

Heskett, J, *Industrial Design*, Thames and Hudson, London, 1980.

Levey, M, *London Transport Posters*, Phaidon, London, 1976.

Lynam, R, *Paris Fashion*, Michael Joseph, London, 1972.

MacGowan, K, *Behind the Screen*, Delacorte Press, New York, 1965.

Meadmore, C, *The Modern Chair*, Van Nostrand Rheinhold Company, London, 1979.

Meikle, J L, *Twentieth Century Limited; Industrial Design in America 1925-39*, Temple University Press, Philadelphia, 1979.

Mouron, H, *Cassandre*, Thames and Hudson, London, 1985.

Nobbs, G, *The Wireless Stars*, Wensum Books, Norwich, 1972.

Pawley, E, *BBC Engineering 1922-72*, BBC Books, London, 1972.

Pevsner, N, *Pioneers of Modern Design*, Harmondsworth, London, 1960.

Phillips, L (ed), *High Style; 20th Century American Design*, Summit Books, Whitney Museum of American Art, New York, 1985.

Raulet, S, *Art Deco Jewellery*, Thames and Hudson, London, 1985.

Whitford, F, *Bauhaus*, Thames and Hudson, London, 1984.

Whittick, A, *European Architecture in the 20th Century*, Leonard Hill, England, 1972.

Wilson, R G, *The Machine Age in America*, Metropolitan Museum of Art, New York, 1986.

ACKNOWLEDGEMENTS

Key: *l* = left; *r* = right; *t* = top;
b = bottom; *c* = centre.

Air Ministry: page 27 *t*. Aldus Archive: page 69. Ian Allen: page 28/29. Aram Design Ltd: page 68 *t*. Architectural Association: pages 8, 35, 47, 49, 52 *t*, 53 *t*. Bettmann Archives: pages 118, 121. Bridgeman Art Library: pages 17, 82; 58 *t* (Egyptian National Museum, Cairo); 86/87, 88 (Victoria & Albert Museum, London); 90/91 (John Jesse, London); 94/95 (Austen Cooper); 98, 105, 109 (Paul Bremen Collection, USA). British Architectural Library/RIBA: pages 110, 113 *t*, 114–117, 120. © Christies, London: pages 9 *b*, 10 *t*, 56/57, 59, 64, 67, 81 102 *t*. © Christies, New York: page 74/75. Design Council: pages 16, 30, 30/31 *t*, 46

b, 68 *b*, 74 *l*, 79. Alistair Duncan: pages 63 (photo Randy Jester); 73 (collection John P Alexrod). Liz Eddison: page 61 *b*. E T Archive: page 76. Mary Evans Picture Library: pages 12, 21. Vivien Fifield Picture Library: pages 80, 103. Geffrye Museum: pages 23, 48 *t*. Giraudon: page 83. Harrah Auto Collection: page 29. Angelo Hornak Photograph Library: pages 6, 8/9 *t*, 11, 18, 43, 50–51, 54, 57 *r*, 58 *b*, 61 *t*, 62, 74/75 *b*, 84, 92, 97. Hulton Picture Library: pages 14/15, 27 *b*, 28 *b*, 37–38, 39 *b*, 104, 112. David King Collection: page 78. The Kobal Collection: pages 30/31 *b*, 32, 36, 39 *t*, 40–41, 96. London Transport Museum: page 85. John

Margolies ESTO: page 10 *b*. The National Motor Museum, Beaulieu: page 24. Robert Opie: pages 22, 93, 107. Chris Pearce/The Vintage Jukebox Company, London: page 42. Quarto Publishing plc/Patricia Bayer: pages 108, 113 *b*. Peter Roberts: page 15. © Trustees of the Science Museum: page 20. Sotheby's, London: pages 44, 48 *b*, 60, 66, 70–72. Tate Gallery, London: pages 46 *t*. Ed Teitelman: page 52/53 *b*. Walter Dorwin Teague Associates: page 119. Gerald Wells, Vintage Wireless Museum, Dulwich: page 34.